W9-CZY-992

THE MISSOURI
R E V I E W

Volume XXVI Number 3   2003

University of Missouri–Columbia

EDITOR
Speer Morgan

MANAGING EDITOR
Hoa Ngo

ASSOCIATE EDITOR
Evelyn Somers

POETRY EDITOR
Bern Mulvey

MARKETING
Kristine Somerville

OFFICE MANAGER
Dedra Earl

EDITORIAL ASSISTANTS
Richard Sonnenmoser and Anthony Varallo

OFFICE ASSISTANTS
Jessica LeTourneur, Ellen Urton, Jamie Wallace

SENIOR ADVISORS
Scott Kaukonen and Jackie Weber

ADVISORS
Steve Gehrke, Megan Jones, Kim Karels, Aaron McClintic,
Michael Piafsky, Nick Sawin, Rachel Weiner

INTERNS
Neha Aggarwal, Morgan Cook, Becky Gerding, Charlie Green,
Cody Meirick, Nathan Oates, Shaen Pogue, Amy Wilkinson

Cartoons in this issue by Jen Sorensen

The Missouri Review is published by the College of Arts & Science of the University of Missouri–Columbia, with private contributions and assistance from the Missouri Arts Council and the National Endowment for the Arts.

The editors invite submissions of poetry, fiction and essays of a general literary interest with a distinctly contemporary orientation. Manuscripts will not be returned unless accompanied by a stamped, self-addressed envelope. Please address all correspondence to The Editors, *The Missouri Review*, 1507 Hillcrest Hall, University of Missouri, Columbia, Missouri, 65211.

Web site at http://www.missourireview.com/

SUBSCRIPTIONS
1 year (3 issues), $22.00
2 years (6 issues), $38.00
3 years (9 issues), $48.00

Copyright © 2003 by The Curators of the University of Missouri
ISSN 0191 1961   **ISBN** 1-879758-39-3
Printed by Thomson-Shore Inc.   Distributed by Ingram Periodicals
Indexed in the American Humanities Index

THE MISSOURI
R E V I E W

XXVI, 3
2003

POETRY (continued)

ESSAYS

BOOK REVIEWS

© 2003 Jen Sorensen

The Pirate Publishers

Something that Bill Bradley asks Tobias Wolff in this issue's interview calls to my mind an embarrassing moment in *The Missouri Review*'s past.

Wolff's new novel, *Old School,* concerns, among other things, an instance of plagiarism. Some ten years ago, a writer sent us a story plagiarized from two authors—Thom Jones and Tobias Wolff. It was a well-cobbled-together forgery using the plot of Wolff's "The Rich Brother" and certain paragraphs directly lifted from Jones's "A White Horse." We were fooled and delighted to publish it. Needless to say, we were less than delighted when we had to apologize in a subsequent issue for having unintentionally played a part in a case of plagiarism. It's a telling note regarding both Wolff and Jones that when I notified them about what had happened, both were concerned for the magazine first. Wolff was also sorry for the writer so desperate for publication that he'd resorted to copying other writers' work.

This is reminiscent of a larger embarrassment in American publishing history. Plagiarism and its near relative, piracy, play a surprisingly large role in the chronicle of book publishing in America. They are a little-discussed ghost in the attic of the industry and one of the reasons why it has such an uninspired history. From the beginning the absence of international copyright law and America's long-lingering sense of cultural inferiority encouraged American printers to simply steal the books of foreign writers. It was cheaper, easier and less risky than putting out original books; on the other hand, relying on stolen goods was not an incentive to relevancy, quality or the development of editorial skills. It also discouraged publication of American authors. Instead of risk-taking, venturesome entrepreneurs looking to the future, pirate publishers were small-time thieves doing whatever it took to make a nickel.

Nineteenth-century magazines on both sides of the Atlantic also engaged in piracy and plagiarism, with some stolen articles and stories bouncing around like ping-pong balls. However, the magazine industry was more vital and technologically sophisticated than the book business, partly because serial production required magazines to be innovative.

Following the Civil War, magazines began to enjoy increased circulations and unprecedented amounts of revenue from advertising. One result was that they paid writers well. The sums paid for stories by the larger-circulation magazines from 1900 through World War II sound substantial even now. Many of the great novels of the late 19th century were delivered to readers serially in successive issues of magazines such as *The Atlantic Monthly* and *Harper's*. Even as late as the 1940s, magazines continued to be more important to writers' incomes than the perennially lackluster, low-paying book market.

Transatlantic literary theft burned up productive writers like Charles Dickens and Mark Twain. Both authors had so many problems with publishers that they started their own publishing operations and spent considerable effort running them. Dickens campaigned for effective international copyright law on one of his American tours, which went over badly with audiences. Americans were either indifferent to such technicalities or took the position that no one "owns" words simply because he or she has spoken, written or even published them. In 1870, a judge used this reasoning in his finding against plaintiff Harriet Beecher Stowe when she sought restitution from a German-language press that had pirated and translated *Uncle Tom's Cabin* for immigrant German speakers. This case notoriously riled American writers. Even when the U.S. finally joined an international agreement in 1891, the period of copyright coverage was so brief that many felt it scarcely served any purpose. A few years later, Twain sarcastically dismissed the handling of copyright: "Whenever a copyright law is to be made or altered, then the idiots assemble."

Yet the reliance on foreign books did begin to change after the copyright agreement of 1891, gradually turning a mostly negative influence on the industry into a mixed one. The rights on books during the first several decades of copyright were typically inexpensive, and cheap foreign books continued to support the new American publishing houses of the 20th century. Publishers still depended on them. However, buying foreign rights instead of simply stealing them had a beneficial effect on everyone concerned, including those who were doing the paying.

When Bennett Cerf and Donald Klopfer bought the Modern Library from Charles Boni in 1925, its list included the usual odd ragbag of books gotten cheap or for nothing from Europe, including three titles by Maeterlinck and six novels by Anatole France—a detail that Klopfer remembered in an interview that appeared in this magazine eighteen years ago (*TMR*, VIII, 1). The two young partners rightly thought that it was a haphazard list and began to pare it down. They continued to get many of their new titles from Europe by making annual visits to favorite European houses. However, they attended more carefully than earlier publishers to the quality and relevance of their lists. Because some of the titles they wanted to buy didn't fit into the idea of the Modern Library, in 1929 they started—for lack of a better idea for a name—"Random House." The quintessential new American publisher of the 20th century was cut from a modified but improved version of the old pattern. If the price they paid for a book was low, at least it wasn't outright piracy, and this financial accountability had a rationalizing influence both on the literature itself and on the industry.

Alfred A. Knopf, established in the same era, operated in a similar way. From the start Knopf relied on books first published elsewhere, sales tested and—until very recent years—purchased at bargain prices. Throughout its history, this prestigious house has been as much a re-publisher as a publisher of original material. Its first book was the English best-seller *Green Mansions* by W. H. Hudson. Like the partners at Random House, Alfred and Blanche Knopf regularly visited England and Europe to look for new titles. In the following years, Knopf editors continued to scan the lists of overseas publishers for possible buys. English houses, such as Heinemann's and Jonathan Cape, were especially good sources. Knopf sought and generally chose quality books, but the bottom line of their editors' evaluations of potential new books, domestic or foreign, was evidence of sales. They were risk averse and conservative in their choices. "Fifty-dollar-a-pound caviar," editor W. H. Weinstock called Borges's best stories in 1949. He admired Borges, but after all, this was the stuff of obscure South American literary magazines, not fiction for a large audience. Knopf had a second crack at buying a collection by Borges eight years later, after he had published several more stories in American literary magazines, but still they turned him down. The collection would be at best a *"succès d'estime,"* said the reader, but it wouldn't sell copies.

It is also clear from their readers' evaluations that Knopf generally avoided controversial subjects. In this magazine (XXIII, 3), we printed the internal readers' reports by Knopf editors of such books as James Baldwin's *Giovanni's Room* ("An unhappy, talented, and repellant book"), Sylvia Plath's *The Bell Jar* ("certainly isn't enough genuine talent for us to take notice"), Jean Rhys's *Wide Sargasso Sea* ("at most, a sort of cultish interest, from secret lovers of the gothic"), and Anaïs Nin's *A Spy in the House of Love*. Blanche Knopf sent only a brief note to the French agent who'd sent her a copy of *Lolita*, saying, "You and I both know this was impossible at least for us. . . . I wonder if any publisher will buy it?" After more than a dozen American publishers turned it down, someone finally did buy *Lolita*—Walter Minton of

G. P. Putnam, in one of those crazy bets that publishers sometimes make and that keep literature alive. Since then, the book has become, if anything, more controversial than it was in the 1950s; it has also sold an estimated fifty million copies worldwide.*

When Random House bought Knopf in the 1960s, it was the model for what became a wave of buyouts and mergers that by the 1990s had become a tsunami threatening to crush what little variety remained in the industry. Paradoxically, this trend toward "going big" is another instance of the industry thinking small. Fretting about risk and complaining that they are engaged in an "impossible business" (the title of a *New Yorker* article about trade publishing, October 6, 1997) with low profit margins and declining unit sales, publishers contend that they have no choice but to sell out to conglomerates. Unfortunately, their problems have only been considerably worsened by this trend.

Trade publishing can't thrive within conglomerates whose founding companies began in cable television, entertainment production, newspaper chains, the whiskey business or even foreign publishing. These business cultures aren't going to fix their problems with "increased market clout," production consolidation, "synergy," "management solutions" or any of the other magical-sounding nostrums supposedly provided by the larger companies. Instead of solving the core problems facing publishers, what conglomerates bring is firings, consolidation, "managers" taking over as editors, inept marketing and the push to shovel out more genre books and turn authors into brand names with "predictable sales," like so many bottles of soft drink. At best these are nickel-and-dime improvements affecting a quarter's balance sheet; at worst they further erode reputations and the morale of employees. In the end, nobody's happy, since the trade publishing units of conglomerates have become their least profitable, least prestigious holdings—a serious comedown for expensive companies bought to serve as showcase properties.

I doubt that the business improvements crucial for publishers' futures will be found by top-heavy companies locked into methods of book production and delivery that have remained unchanged for over sixty years; instead, they will have to come from the sort of audacity most recently seen in technology companies. I could foresee changes involving flexible-print-run book delivery, along with variable formatting and binding options that include high-quality (and high-margin) books. Also, the business might benefit by undergoing a split similar to the software/hardware division in technology, in which editing specialists or houses develop books and then license them to producer distributors. Producers could then concentrate their efforts on making books and delivering them in ways that provide alternatives to an outdated wholesale-retail system. These changes would open up the field for new and potentially high-quality editing imprints (with low capitalization requirements), as well as unleashing other talent in everything from writing to printing and sales.

However it's done, entrepreneurs have to find ways to transcend a system that historically has lacked vision and nerve—a system that currently marks every book selling less than twenty or twenty-five thousand copies as "disappointments." Too many relatively successful and highly regarded books end up handicapping editors' and authors' careers. Something is wrong in a business that generates this much failure.

The more important solution for trade publishers has less to do with business, though, than with finding and presenting good and occasionally great books. Publishers need to put more energy into looking for great *individual* books. Rather than eking out their survival on genre, celebrity, diet, and general junk, they should put more effort into looking for those singular books that make a difference, the ones that make them proud to be editors, redound to their reputations as publishers and may just sell beyond anyone's imagining.

Despite the quagmire of megamedia publishing, fine writers do manage to achieve reputations and survive. The ways they do so vary from case to case but include literary magazine and university-press publication, which is particularly important to early-career and noncommercial authors, such as short-story writers and poets. International publication is also important. Translated writing from places like Latin America has been widely influential in the last thirty years. British publishers have introduced some of the best English-language writers of the past few decades, including V. S. Naipaul, Salman Rushdie and J. M. Coetzee. *The Missouri Review* has published or interviewed such writers as Stanislaw Lem, Naguib Mahfouz, Chinua Achebe, Mario Vargas Llosa and others. Many of the stories in this issue concern international issues.

It is an interesting note on the saga of copyright that as writers have begun to be more reasonably compensated for foreign rights, with extended periods of coverage and better protection against piracy, literature has become more truly international. In a world fractured by politics and war, this is a good thing.

SM

*The full Knopf files are at the Harry Ransom Center at the University of Texas at Austin

©2003 Jen Sorensen

Accidental Hipsters

ELEANOR McMURTRY, 67

RETIRED BOOKKEEPER

IN QUEST FOR A COMFORTABLE PAIR OF WALKING SHOES, UNWITTINGLY PURCHASED EXTREMELY HIP, 1975-REISSUE NYLON CONVERSE TRAINERS.

JAMES GOODBEARD, 48

CLASSICS PROFESSOR

DESIRING WARM WINTER OUTERWEAR, BOUGHT MASSIVELY PUFFY TOMMY HILFIGER DOWN JACKET, WHOLLY UNAWARE OF ITS URBAN CHIC SYMBOLISM.

SARAH SANDERS, 19

COLLEGE STUDENT

SPORTS DEAD KENNEDYS T-SHIRT OUT OF CONFUSION, THINKING "DK" LOGO STANDS FOR DELTA KAPPA SORORITY TO WHICH SHE BELONGS.

JACK BERGER, 56

YAM FARMER

TRAGICALLY UNCONSCIOUS OF FACT THAT ENTIRE WARDROBE IS A GOLD MINE OF PROLETARIAT KITSCH HIGHLY COVETED BY IRONIC TWENTY-SOMETHINGS.

www.slowpokecomics.com

Jen Sorensen is the creator of Slowpoke, a weekly comic strip which appears in several alternative papers nationwide, as well as the *Funny Times*. Sorensen's freelance illustrations have appeared in *Nickelodeon*, *Legal Affairs* and other magazines. More of her cartoons can be found at www.slowpokecomics.com.

THE EDGE OF THE WORLD / *Alice Hoffman*

1778

I.

It was said that boys should go on their first sea voyage at the age of ten, but surely this notion was never put forth by anyone's mother. If the bay were to be raised one degree in temperature for every woman who had lost the man or child she loved at sea, the water would have been boiling, throwing off steam even in the dead of winter, poaching the bluefish and herrings as they swam.

Every May, the women in town gathered at the wharf. No matter how beautiful the day, scented with apple blossoms or new grass or spring onions, they found themselves wishing for snow and ice, for gray November, for December's gales and landlocked harbors, for fleets that returned safe and sound, all hands accounted for, all boys grown into men. Women who had never left Massachusetts dreamed of the Middle Banks and the Great Banks the way some men dreamed of hell: the place that could give you everything you might need and desire. The place that could take it all away.

This year the fear of what might be was worse than ever, never mind gales and storms and starvation and accidents, never mind rum and arguments and empty nets. This year the British had placed an embargo on the ships of the cape. No one could go in or out of the harbor, except unlawfully, which is what the fishermen in town planned to do come May, setting off on moonless nights, a few sloops at a time, with the full knowledge that every man caught would be put to death for treason and every boy would be sent to Dartmoor Prison in England—as good as death, people in town agreed, but colder and more miserable.

Most people were accounted for, those who would go and those who would stay behind to man the fort beside Long Pond if need be, a battle station that was more of a cabin than anything, but at least it was something solid to lean against should a man have to take aim and fire. John Hadley was among those who wanted to stay. He made that clear, and everyone knew he had his reasons. He had just finished the little house in the hollow that he'd been working on with his older son, Vincent, for nearly three years. During this time, he and Vincent had gone out fishing only for the month of May, searching out bluefish and halibut, fish large enough so that you could fill up your catch in a very short time. John's sloop was small, his desires few: he wanted to give his wife this house, nothing fancy, but carefully made all the same, along with the acreage around it, a meadow filled with wild grapes and winterberry. Wood for building was hard to come by, so John had used old wrecked boats for the joists, deadwood he'd found in the shipyard, and when there was none of that to be had, he used fruitwood he'd culled from his property, though people insisted such apple wood and pear wouldn't last. There was no glass in the windows, only oiled paper, but the light that came through was dazzling and yellow; little flies buzzed in and out of the light, and everything seemed slow, molasses slow, lovesick slow. John Hadley felt a deep love for his wife, Coral, more so than anyone might guess. He was still tongue-tied in her presence, and he had the foolish notion that he could give her something no one else could. Something precious and lasting and hers alone. It was the house he had in mind whenever he looked at Coral. This was what love was to him: when he was at sea he could not sleep without the feel of her beside him. She was his anchor; she was his home; she was the road to everything that mattered to John Hadley.

Otis West and his cousin Harris Mcquire had helped with the plans for the house—a keeping room, an attic for the boys, a separate chamber for John and Coral. These men were good neighbors, and they'd helped again when the joists were ready, even though they both thought John was a fool for giving up the sea. A man didn't give up who he was just to settle down. He didn't trade his freedom for turnips. Still, these neighbors spent day after day working alongside John and his son, Vincent, bringing their oxen along to help lift the cross beams, hollering for joy when the heart of the work was done, ready to get out the good rum. The town was like that: for or against you, people helped each other out. Even old Margaret Swift, who was foolish enough to have raised the British flag on the pole outside her house, was politely served when she came into the general store, though there were folks in town who believed that by rights she should be drinking tar and spitting feathers.

John's older son, Vincent, was a big help in the building of the house, just as he was out at sea, and because of this they would soon be able to move out of the rooms they let at Hannah Crosby's house. But Isaac, who had just turned ten, was not quite so helpful. He meant to be, but he was still a child, and he'd recently found a baby blackbird that kept him busy. Too busy for other chores, it seemed. First, he'd had to feed the motherless creature every hour with crushed worms and johnnycake crumbs; then he'd had to drip water into the bird's beak from the tip of his finger. He'd started to hum to the blackbird, as if it were a real baby. He'd started to talk to it when he thought no one could overhear.

"Wild creatures belong in the wild," Coral Hadley told her son. All the same, she had difficulty denying Isaac anything. Why, she'd let the boy smuggle his pet into their rooms at the Crosbys', where he kept the blackbird in a wooden box beside his bed.

The real joy of the house for John was that it was indeed a farm. They would have cows and horses to consider, rather than halibut and blue-fish: predictable beasts at long last, and a large and glorious and pre-dictable meadow as well. Rather than the cruel ocean, there would be fences and a barn and a deep cistern of cold well water, the only water John's boys would need or know, save for the pond at the rear of the property, where damselflies glided above the mallows in spring. John Hadley had begun to talk about milk cows and crops. He'd become fascinated with turnips, how hardy they were, how easy to grow, even in sandy soil. In town, people laughed at him. John Hadley knew this, and he didn't care. He'd traveled far enough in his lifetime. Once, he'd been gone to the island of Nevis all summer long with the Crosbys on their schooner; he'd brought Coral back an emerald, he'd thought that was what she wanted most in the world. But she'd told him to sell it and buy land. She knew that was what he wanted.

Coral was a good woman, and John was a handsome man, tall, with dark hair and darker eyes, a Cornishman, as tough as men from Corn-wall always were. All the same, he didn't have too much pride to herd sheep or clean out a stable or plant corn and turnips, though it meant a long-term battle with brambles and nettle. Still, his was a town of fish-ermen. Like soldiers who can never leave their country once they've buried their own in the earth, so here it was the North Atlantic that called to them, a graveyard for sure, but home just as certainly. And John was still one of them, at least for the present time. If a man in these parts needed to earn enough to buy fences, cows and turnips, he knew where he had to go. It would only be from May to July, John figured, and that would be the end of it, especially if he was helped by his two strong sons.

They moved into the house in April, on a pale calm day when the buds on the lilacs their neighbors had planted as a welcome were just about to unfold. The house was finished enough to sleep in; there was a fireplace where Coral could cook, and the rest would come eventu-ally. Quite suddenly, John and Coral felt as though time was unlimited, that it was among the things that would never be in short supply.

"That's where the horses will be," John Hadley told Coral. They were looking out over the field that belonged to them, thanks to those years

John had spent at sea and the emerald they'd sold. "I'll name one Charger. I had a horse called that when I was young." Coral laughed to think of him young. She saw her boys headed for the pond. The blackbird chick rode on Isaac's shoulder and flapped his wings. It was their first day, the beginning of everything. Their belongings were still in crates.

"I'll just take him with me and Vincent this one time," John said. "I promise. Then we'll concentrate on turnips."

"No," Coral said. She wanted three milk cows and four sheep and her children safe in their own beds. She thought about her youngest, mashing worms into paste for his fledgling. "Isaac can't go."

By then the brothers had reached the shores of the little pond. The frogs jumped away as they approached. The blackbird, frightened by the splashing, hopped into the safety of Isaac's shirt and sent out a small muffled cry.

"He's like a hen," the older brother said. At fifteen, Vincent had grown to his full height, six foot, taller than his father; he was full of himself and how much he knew. He'd been to sea twice, after all, and he figured he knew as much as any man; he already had calluses on his hands. He didn't need to go to school anymore, which was just as well, since he'd never been fond of his lessons. "He doesn't even know he can fly," Vincent said of his brother's foundling.

"I'll teach him." Isaac felt in his shirt for the blackbird. The blackbird reminded him of water, soft and cool. Sometimes he let the bird sleep right beside him, on the quilt his mother had sewn out of indigo homespun.

"Nah, you won't. He's a big baby, just like you are. He'll be walking around on your shoulder for the rest of his life."

After that, Isaac brought the blackbird into the woods every day, just to prove Vincent wrong. He climbed into one of the tall oaks and let his legs dangle over a high limb. He urged the blackbird to fly away, but the bird was now his pet, too attached to ever leave; the poor thing merely paced on his shoulder and squawked. Isaac decided to name his pet Ink. He was an indoor bird, afraid of the wind and of others of his own kind. He hopped around the parlor and nested beneath the wood stove, where it was so hot he singed his feathers. He sat on the table and sipped water from a saucer while Isaac did his studies. It was a navigation book Isaac was studying, *The Practical Navigator*. If he was not as strong as Vincent or as experienced, then at least he could memorize the chart of the stars; he could know the latitude of where they were going and where they'd been.

"Do you think I could teach him to talk?" Isaac said dreamily to his mother one day. Ink was perched on the tabletop, making a nuisance of himself.

"What would a blackbird have to say?" Coral laughed.

"He'd say: *I'll never leave you. I'll be with you for all time.*"

Coral said she needed some air. She went into the yard and faced the meadow. She looked at the way the tall grass moved in the wind. That night she said to her husband again, "Don't take him with you, John."

April was ending, with sheets of rain and the sound of the peepers calling from the shore of the pond. Classes would end in a few days, too—they called it a fisherman's school. Boys were free to be sent out to work with their fathers or uncles or neighbors from May till October. The Hadleys left in the first week of that mild month, a night when there was no moon. The fog had come in—so much the better, when it came to sneaking away. The British had lookouts to the east and the west, and it was best to take a northerly route. They brought along molasses, the fishing nets, johnnycake and salted pork, and, unknown to John and Vincent, Isaac took along his blackbird as well, tucked into his jacket. As they rounded the turn out of their own harbor, Isaac took his pet from his hiding place.

"You could do it now if you wanted to," he said to the bird. "You could fly away."

But the blackbird shivered in the wind, startled, it seemed, by the sound of water. He scrambled back to the safety of Isaac's jacket, feathers puffed up, the way they always were when he was frightened.

"I told you he'd never fly." Vincent had spied the blackbird. He nudged his brother so that Isaac would help check the nets. "He's pathetic, really."

"No, he's not!"

By now they were past the fog that always clung to shore at this time of year, and the night was clear; there were so many stars in the sky that the vast expanse of dark and light was frightening. The water was rougher then Isaac had ever seen it in their bay, and they were still not even halfway to the Middle Banks. The sloop seemed small out here, far too breakable.

"Is this the way it always is?" Isaac asked his brother. He felt sick to his stomach; there was a lurching in his bones and blood. He thought about the oak tree and the meadow and the frogs and the way his mother looked at him when he came in through the door. "It's the way it is tonight," Vincent said.

Used to the sea, Vincent fell asleep easily, but Isaac couldn't close his eyes. John Hadley understood; he came to sit beside the boy. It was so dark that every star in the sky hung suspended above the mast, as though only inches above them. Isaac recognized the big square of Pegasus that he'd seen in his book. The night looked like spilled milk, and John Hadley pointed out Leo, the harbinger of spring, and the North Star, constant as always. John could hear the chattering of the blackbird in his son's waistcoat. He could taste his wife's farewell kiss.

"What happens if a storm comes up?" Isaac said, free to be frightened now that his brother was asleep, free to be the boy that he was. "What happens if I'm thrown overboard? Or if a whale comes along? What happens then?"

"Then I'll save you," John Hadley said. When the wind changed he smelled turnips; he really did, and he laughed at the scent, how it had followed him all this way to the Middle Banks to remind him of everything he had to lose.

II.

So many men were taken in the May gale that the Methodist Church on Main Street could not hold all the relatives of the lost all on one day. There was a full week of services, and not a single body to behold. The law suggested three months pass by before a service was held; time after time, it was true, sailors who had been thrown off course by the cruel circumstances of the seas and assumed drowned had appeared at their own funerals. When a drowned man arrived on the steps of the church, those who mourned him demanded to know where on earth he'd been all this time. Was there another woman in the West Indies or up in Nova Scotia? Had every cent he'd earned at sea been spent on rum? The truth was usually far simpler: it took a long time to get back home, out here to the edge of the world.

After the May gale the town waited an unheard-of six months before the services commenced, and even then Coral Hadley refused to have her husband and sons counted among those who were mourned. She didn't answer the door when the parson came to call; she didn't attend a single one of the services, though they were held for the husbands and sons of her friends, Harris Mcquire and Otis West among them. Coral had known something would happen the morning they'd left. That was the worst part of it: she kept going back to that day, wondering what might have been if only she'd insisted on having her way. She'd found four blue eggs out on the hillock by the pond, and every egg had a hole in it. Coral had rattled each one. Nothing inside. A bad sign to find such things, a terrible sign, an omen of misfortune and of lives unfinished, unspooled. Later that night, when the wind came up, she heard her name called aloud. When she told people about this, no one believed her, but Coral didn't care. She'd gone to stand outside the night when they disappeared; though it was foggy, she went into the field where they would keep their cows, where the horse they planned to name Charger would graze, and she heard someone say, *I'll never leave you.*

As soon as news of the gale came in, she refused to mourn with the other women. Right away she said there'd be no service, no matter what the parson advised, and months later she still could not be moved. The women in town tried to convince her for months to let the dead be put to rest; they'd seen women in a mourning delirium before, unable to tell what was real and what was not. Even old Hannah Crosby came down the lane and told Coral she had to face up to the terrible thing that had happened. If the British had caught her men, they surely would have heard by now; John would have been taken to trial in Boston, just like the Henry brothers and so many others. There would have been some news of the boys.

"I can wait," Coral said. That and nothing more.

She started to plant the field, the way she thought John would want her to. She dug in row after row of turnips, and then she planted corn, and at last she sprinkled the seed pods of pink sweet peas, feed for the cows they would someday have, and for remembrance as well. John had favored sweet peas and had brought her armfuls of the flowers when he was courting her. Her mother had said they were weeds, but as was often the case, her mother was wrong.

Coral worked with a pick in the hot sun all summer long, unafraid of dirt or hard work, dressed in black, refusing to eat anything her neighbors might bring. She thought of her family, lost at sea, and in their honor ate only johnnycakes and catfish caught from the pond, which she simmered in an old pan over the wood stove. She kept in mind those men who had reappeared at their own funerals: Robert Servich and Nathaniel Hawkes, for instance, both of them lost for months in the Indies and now living right down the lane. She thought about turnip stew and turnip cakes and how pleased John would be when he tasted the fruit of her labors. How he'd be surprised to hear there were green onions growing wild near the far field, that there was a grapevine so huge it would keep them in jellies and jams and pies all year long.

And then, the next spring, when May had arrived and the leaves were budding in shades of yellow and green, Coral realized that the blackbird had returned. It took some time before she recognized it because the bird had turned entirely white. It sat in a branch of the big oak, where it could have easily been mistaken for a wisp of a cloud. It looked like something Coral could blink away, but it wouldn't disappear. First the bird was on her roof, then it was at her window, and then one morning the white blackbird tapped at the door, and that was how she knew they were gone.

In an instant she knew everything she had hoped for was gone. She cut off all her hair and she tore the clothes she wore with a carving knife. She threw away her frying pan and her kettle, her spices and her liberty tea, all tossed right into the pond. She might have starved to death if Hannah Crosby hadn't seen that bird circling over the property like a vulture or a ghost. The doctor was called in; some sassafras tea and bed rest was recommended. Hannah, to her credit, suggested that Coral come back and live in the lodging rooms the family had occupied before John built the house, but she could tell, with one harsh look from Coral, that the answer was no.

In another town, a widow's vandu might be suggested and a year of Coral's labor put up for auction, but this was not the sort of place where people were sold to the highest bidder. The Hawkes family brought over an old cow that was still a good milker, and Hannah Crosby was happy to oversee the garden to insure there'd be a decent crop of turnips, if nothing else.

By the end of the summer, Coral Hadley was selling her turnips by the side of the road, set out in crates, trusting folks' honesty. The turnips were particularly large; one alone could last a week. People said they were so sweet a single bite could bring a man to tears.

Buyers tended to leave more money in the cash box than they needed to. Even the British soldiers took three boxes of turnips along with them for their voyage home, and they left Coral Hadley eight shillings per box, far more than such things were worth.

Seven years after the May gale, the white blackbird could still be spied. It was said Coral Hadley had tried to chase it off; she'd fired a musket at it, she'd thrown a bucket of ashes in its direction, but it wouldn't go away. Even after all these years, people remembered her suffering. Perhaps her neighbors thought it was luck to help the luckless: some of the men put up a fence around Coral's garden and another one around the barn. One spring a pair of sheep was left in her field. Another May, a dusty gray horse that looked very much like one belonging to the Mcquire family was tied up to the post outside the house. People took to leaving out food for the bird as well, crumb cakes and molasses bread, for that was said to be good luck too. Hannah Crosby, who so feared birds, left morsels on a stump in the center of the meadow and swore that the blackbird had eaten from the palm of her hand.

One summer day, Coral Hadley went out early to feed the sheep and the cow and the horse she had named Charger, and there was a man in her yard. Each spring she had planted sweet peas; now they were everywhere, knee high, blossoming, purple and white and pink. Coral knew she wasn't the person she used to be: her teeth were falling out, ground down by nightmares; her hair had turned white. People in town said she was hurrying her old age, rushing forward to meet her husband, John, and her children in the hereafter, but really she was rushing toward this moment, this instant, this very breath.

The May gale had surprised them, as it had surprised everyone else who was fishing in the Middle Banks. One moment there'd been a sea of glass, the next a sea of mountains. They did the best any crew could have done. Even Isaac managed as well as could be expected, as they'd tried to drive leeward. But in the force of the storm, the sloop broke apart and there was nothing any crew might have done. It had happened not slowly but all at once, as though a giant had picked them up and crushed them with a single stroke. Everything splintered; everything broke; everything was devoured by the sea. Things that couldn't be were. Things that should never have happened were there before their eyes. Vincent knew how bad it was when his brother threw the blackbird into the sky, threw him with both hands, a last, desperate act of love.

John Hadley's final act was to roll the molasses barrel to Vincent so he could float with it. John grabbed his younger son around the chest, and he and Isaac disappeared almost at once. To his great shame, Vincent clung to the barrel. That was how the British schooner found him; they'd had to pry his frozen fingers from the metal band around the center. Though they were enemies and had no choice but to take him to Dartmoor Prison, the soldiers congratulated him on his fortitude. They did not ask if he'd been at sea all alone, and he did not tell them that he had watched his father and his brother drown. If that was fortitude, it was something he didn't care to possess. If that was strength, he wanted none of it. He wished he'd let go of that barrel that had saved him.

Vincent Hadley had been in prison in England for three years, until the war was over, and then he was released without a shilling. Prison had been a strange dream of hearing other men talk and rant and list their regrets. As for Vincent, he never said much, although it was evident that he had regrets as well. He'd cried for the first year, pathetically, horribly, and then he had stopped. By the time he was released he probably could not have cried if he'd been stabbed right through his chest. There was no water left inside him.

He got the only work he felt capable of doing, signing on to one ship after another, always checking for a route that might bring him closer to home. Another man might have carried with him a justified fear of the sea; he might have lived in dread of storms a man couldn't fight and gales that came up suddenly at the hour when the sea seemed calm as glass. But in fact, Vincent was fearless. If something dangerous needed to be done, he need simply be asked, not even commanded. He would dive into the coldest tide and scrape barnacles from beneath a sloop. He would retrieve anchors from the deep. He would wrestle with bluefish, and he had the marks of their teeth on his arms to show that although he'd won many fights, the battles had been fierce.

At last he got to Virginia. He was a man of twenty-two by then, and he still didn't talk much. He had no answers, and he wanted no questions. He'd spent so much time in the West Indies that his blood had thinned; he was no longer used to the cold, and he knew that as he traveled it would get colder still. The first thing he did after arriving in Virginia was to buy a deerskin jacket. The second thing he did was to start to work his way north, always fishing, always taking the most dangerous of jobs. Whenever the men he worked alongside said go back, whenever the sea was at its worst, Vincent said go forward. He considered writing a letter home explaining where he'd been, but he'd never been much for writing, and when it came down to it, what did he have to say? That the blackbird had dipped its wings into the cold, roiling sea where it was covered in foam? That he'd guessed it would drown, but instead it had suddenly flown upward, that pet of his brother's that had never before taken flight? It had disappeared into a cloud.

It took him seven years to think of what he would say. He was a tall, handsome, quiet man; he took after his father in some ways. Women fell in love with him, but he wasn't concerned with them. He still had the mark of the copper band around the barrel embedded in the skin of his fingers on both hands. Some people said the marks looked like rings, and perhaps that's what they were. He was wedded to something already, and no woman in Virginia or Maryland or New York could tie him to her for longer than a few days.

It was summer when he reached the Cape. He started down the King's Highway, that rutted sandy lane that would take him home. When he stopped at taverns and heard Massachusetts voices, he felt as though he'd been gone far longer than seven years. He wanted to walk and get the feel of the place. He wanted to take his time and see milkweed and wild blueberries and cranberry bogs. He'd been at sea for so long and was so accustomed to its constant motion, it took a while before he got used to solid ground. He slept beneath the oak trees and ordered bread and gravy and little else in the taverns where he occasionally stopped. He had taught himself not to long for water or hunger for food. There wasn't much he was attached to in this world. The bite marks on his arms from the bluefish burned, but he paid the scars no mind. He thought about how sure he'd been of himself, once, how he'd believed he was as knowledgeable as any man. He thought about the damselflies gliding over the pond and the sound of the frogs plashing in the water and the yellow light coming in through the windows of the house his father had built. He thought about how love could move you in ways you wouldn't have imagined, one foot in front of the other, even when you thought you had nothing left inside. He smelled lilacs after a while, and the scent of wild onions. There were the sweet peas, right in front of him, already in bloom, acres of them, grown carefully from seed, a pink-hued and endless sea.

Alice Hoffman is the author of fifteen novels, most recently *The Probable Future*, one book of stories, *Local Girls*, and five books for children, including *Green Angel*. Her new book of stories, which includes *The Edge of the World*, will be published in August by Doubleday.

SERGEANT CROCKER NEWTON RECOLLECTS THE RETURN OF THANE GOULD TO ENDICOTT, MASSACHUSETTS, IN THE WINTER OF 1977/
Brendan Galvin

That was the winter a nameless December hurricane
laid the freighter *Etruria* lengthwise on the sand
at Head of the Meadow, then Thane appeared
in early January as though there was some connection,
hitchhiking down Route 6. Before I saw who it was
I had already pulled the cruiser over to check him out:
short on luggage, jailhouse tattoos on the backs
of his hands, hair to his shoulders and stiff as
peanut brittle, like you could snap it off. And his back
showing signs of defeat, still lugging the invisible piano
of a recent attitude adjustment. A cop's inclination
is to keep a vision like that moving on down the road:
he's probably not in town to visit his dear old mother.
Then I saw it was Cousin Thane, only thinner than
chopsticks and fresh from two years' incarceration
down there in Santa Marijuana or whatever they call it.
Before I let him off at Aunt Shirley's, he'd told me
what a damn fool he was. Gone and gotten in on the deal
because he wanted to go into auto parts, twenty K
they promised him and the other guys apiece on delivery
of the bales up here to Cape Cod, except by the time
they'd anchored overnight at Santa Whatchacallit
the crew was sampling the cargo, and everyone
in port got wind of it. The jailer'd slide a bowl into the cell
and watch them fight for it like chickens in a hen yard.
Fish and rice the whole two years. Of course the pus-bags
who'd signed him up went into thin air, and the moral
of the story is that when Thane did the math—plenty of time
for that between eye-gougings for a few mackerel parts—
he saw he could have saved the twenty grand
by doing oil changes right here in Endicott two years
for Moxie Hogan, or shingling for the Olafsen brothers.
He's been clean ever since. Chopping up the beams
and laths in the house Aunt Shirley left him

to keep warm was dumb, but it wasn't a crime.
All night he leaves the lights on in that little trailer,
even now. Says he gets dizzy in strange buildings.
Things couldn't been too easy in that jailhouse after dark,
I'd say, and anyway a man's got to watch himself.

CATBOAT / *Brendan Galvin*

Year upon year, trial and error:
of a thousand anonymous quahoggers
looking up from low tides, rubbing their backs,
one studying his widow-maker
anchored in the mud is thinking,

Push the width toward the stern
so her beam's half her length
and you've got a broader, flatter deck,
less chance of going ass up.

Then another, scratching the flats
miles and years away: Maybe shove
the mast up closer to her bow and hang
a longer boom for more canvas.
You've got storage up front then—add
a low cabin—and the load's
that much closer to the keel.

The way an idea is layered, her keel's
laid on in strips of fir. Red cedar
lengths, an inch square, bend
to the fit from bow to transom,
until she's like a horseshoe that will float.

Above a life-size blueprint called a lofting,
form is following function now
and forever. When it comes to workboats,
this is one of the shapes necessity evolved,

broad-beamed but shallow,
almost a scallop shell for the hummocks
and shoals of these northern waters,
but stable around the holes and channels,

her one large sail laid on for speed upwind
and down, and to come about
quick when water and sky turn ugly,
and get you to hell home.

A FEW LOCAL NAMES OF THE DOUBLE-CRESTED CORMORANT / *Brendan Galvin*

This is the fish-bird that flew here
directly out of its fossil imprint, unchanged
for sixty million years, hell's turkey
from its punk hairdo to its black rubber
scuba-flipper feet, hanging its wingspread
to dry on rocks and creek banks, crosstrees
of masts, the insignia of a country that has
no plans for peace and no word for civility,
nesting in branches of matted seaweed
this guano goose fixes in a mixture
of its own trashfish paste and pellets,
until the tree surrenders of chagrin
and collapses to poison its pond. It is all
overstatement, stink duck and goo loon,
and can make a buffet of a catfish farmer's
ponds, then slime every deck in the harbor
with the by-product overnight, collateral
damage, its green mineral eyechip
and yellow gawp testimony that it knows
it has thrived beyond dinosaurs
and will slip past even the cockroaches
on its own slicks, this gluebird,
stool pigeon, shag rat.

BLACKTHORN AND ASH / *Brendan Galvin*

Carndonagh, Donegal

Doherty's cows are staring from the next field
in hopes of a rough lick of salt off our palms,
and we are staring at a few tumbled walls,
not even thatched sheds now, slick with
the morning softness off Trawbreaga Bay—
Bryan and Bridget's farmstead in Ballyloskey,
themselves a hundred years in the churchyard
a mile below, among the Tolands and Divers
and Dohertys. So this is the source,
obscured by the ash trees and blackthorns
growing through rooms my grandfather's
mother and father grew their children in,
before the boys caught rides to Moville and took
the lighter out to the Glasgow-Boston steamer
anchored on Lough Foyle, with ash twigs
in their pockets, charms against drowning,
that tree possessing the power resident in water.
Straight as the heart for hayforks and oars, too,
but flexible for the ribbing of curraghs,
and possessed by a poetry of its own:
wind on the deep, moon of the waters, it linked
the inner and outer worlds, clearing the way
of strife. Which would be the precinct
of blackthorn, that strife, wood of the clubs
of faction fighters, its sloe fruit a pucker for satire,
for latter-day Vikings around a kitchen table,
in for tea-time off Loughs Foyle and Swilly
and pressing a crown of those thorns to one
absent forehead or another. Blackthorn and ash,
balanced somehow in those children I remember
white-haired at wakes in their dark suits.

DOGS OF TRURO / *Brendan Galvin*

The first anonymous baying
from those backlit hills petitions a single
greeny-blue winter star.
It silvers as I watch, tuning its sharpness.
Deep January in the natural dark,
and now another to the south is yelping,
Sladesville trying to talk with Prince Valley,
or Corn Hill calling Pond Village across
the cold. This is their time, who have
no heaven unless they create it
with their fierce singing from hogbacks
and down in the evergreen-lined
pockets of the dark. At such ululating,
even the sea hushes and the landscape
turns black and silver—a negative of the day.
This one now may be saying, I am Magnus
of Crow Hill, and here is my story, or Lilith
from Castle Road may be claiming she raised
that moon that's just clearing the trees
toward Ballston. Later the owls will take over,
as by woodstoves and under coffee tables
these yodelers and wailers run their legs
in dreams, but it's sociable for the moment,
contact, contact, a whisker tickling
a crystal of frost, the stars drawing nearer,
a planet turning to listen.

Brendan Galvin is the author of thirteen collections of poems. His recent books are *The Strength of a Named Thing* (1999) and *Sky and Island Light* (1997), both from Louisiana State University Press, and the narrative poem "Hotel Malabar," winner of the 1997 Iowa Poetry Prize (University of Iowa Press, 1998). His translation of Sophocles' *Women of Trachis* appeared in the Penn Greek Drama Series in 1998. LSU Press published *Place of Keepers* in 2003. He lives in Truro, Massachusetts.

DELICATE TOUCH/*Stephanie Waxman*

KAZU TAKAMURA SAT upright on the cream-colored leather couch, which took some effort as the couch was wide and deep, designed to relax people. But Kazu Takamura was not relaxed. He glanced nervously at the secretary again. She sat at a computer, her eyes glued to the screen. She had told him it would only be a few minutes, but that had been fifteen minutes ago.

At least he thought she had indicated a few minutes. Maybe he had misunderstood. Maybe he had not been kept waiting. Maybe his appointment was at four o'clock, not three-thirty. At any rate, several people had passed through the room, and no one had offered him tea.

His thin, tapered fingers reached down once again to touch the large black portfolio resting against his thigh. He glanced at his watch. He brushed an errant thread from his trousers. Once more he looked at the pictures on the wall, black-and-white photos, narrow black wooden frames, off-white 2¾-inch mats. The one of the reclining nude irritated him. The angle of the light on her backside was too obvious. The one of the mountain had a calming effect, and his eyes lingered on it a moment. The way the light danced on the edge of the ridge reminded him of Mount Fuji at dawn. He felt a pang at being so far from home. Just then, the door to the inner office opened, and a woman paused at its threshold. She was of medium height with a sprinkling of brown spots on her face. She wore a plain gray suit, a red silk scarf at her throat. Her hair was the color of udon noodles. He couldn't guess her age; *gaijin* all seemed the same to him.

She walked over to him and extended her hand. "Mr. Takamura."

He couldn't get used to the offer of a hand. He took it limply in his own. Her hand was soft and cool. He let it go quickly. "Much pleasure to meet," he said as he stood.

"I'm Toni Donaldson," she said, her eyes bright and friendly. "I hope your trip was pleasant. I've been so anxious to meet you."

She spoke too fast. He was losing the sense of what she wanted, but when she turned to go back into the office, he followed.

Her office was a quiet room, lit by northern light. Her desk was large and neat. Several paintings leaned against one wall. A bookcase stood against another. There was a black leather couch facing two chairs separated by a low, square glass table. An architect's table stood in front of the window. The whole city spread out below.

"Can I get you a soda? Coffee? Perrier? Here, why don't you take a seat," she said.

He sat down and said with as much politeness as the situation demanded, "Whatever you drink, I will drink."

She gave a quick laugh, saying, "If I have any more caffeine I'll jump out that window!" Then she called through the open door, "Alex, two Perriers."

What was Perrier? In any case, he was pleased to note that in America there were ceremonious exchanges before business.

"So," she said, sliding into the chair facing him, "you are here at last! Somehow I expected you'd be older. Though what can one really tell from e-mails?"

He nodded, searching for a word to say about her age. Finally, he abandoned the effort in favor of a safer topic. "It is very warm today."

"That's for sure. California in March is a real treat if you're used to cold weather. It makes hanging a show so much easier. No tracking muddy slush into the gallery. We'll go over after lunch so you can check out the space. But first, I'm so eager to see everything!"

A young man entered and placed two glasses on the table. "Thanks, Alex," the woman said. The young man left, closing the door behind him. The woman took her glass and stood up. Kazu took his own and was momentarily confused. Were they not going to drink together first, before looking at his work?

He stood, holding his glass.

She took a few gulps, then set her drink down. "We can lay everything out over there," she said, indicating the drafting table.

He made a slight bow and set his glass aside. He certainly wouldn't put it anywhere near his work.

He went to the drafting table, unzipped his portfolio and sat on the high stool facing the table. She stood behind him, peering over his shoulder, so close he could smell her perfume. He wished she would move back, but even if he knew the English words, he would never ask such a thing.

He removed the first painting and carefully laid it down, pleased to note that the table was free of dust. He peeled back the thin film of parchment to reveal *School Children*. Three boys, their schoolbooks scattered to the side of a country road, surrounded a school friend. She was bent forward over a fallen log, her uniform pushed up, her panties down around her knees. Two boys held her arms while a third flogged her bare bottom with the strap that had held his books.

"Such a delicate touch," the woman said. "The line is so subtle; the pigment is barely there." She leaned over his shoulder to better inspect the image. "It's terribly exciting to see the originals at last. What's next?"

Keeping the parchment behind *School Children*, he carefully laid it to one side, then brought out the picture entitled *Old Grandfather*. As in the classic late-19th-century woodcuts of Japanese erotica, it showed a man peeping through a *shoji* screen to view the scene beyond: an old man, skinny and shriveled except for his engorged penis, which was pushed into a woman, her face wide in horror, her kimono torn.

"Ahh," said the woman. "In the tradition of *shunga*, with the peeping-Tom motif. Ingenious."

She knew about *shunga!* Kazu felt himself color at the compliment. So few foreigners understood the historical context of his work.

The next piece was his favorite, *Girl on a Swing*. The ground color was green, the girl done in pale pink, the swing red. She swung high, her pigtails flying. A man, laughing wildly, faced her. His kimono had fallen open, revealing a large erection. The girl had a frantic look on her face as she pumped furiously, the blue tie of her school uniform whipping behind her.

The American woman said nothing. Kazu waited for her to make a comment about the realistic depiction of the landscape. Or to notice the pale color of the girl's skin compared to the darker color of the man. Or perhaps to appreciate the perspective, slightly exaggerated to highlight the central figure. But her silence continued. He did not want to look at her, to indicate in any way that he was waiting. He sat still, hardly breathing.

What if she had had a sudden change of heart? Or worse, what if she had just been humoring him about the other pieces? Perhaps she was now considering how to politely reject everything.

But then she touched his back. He felt violated by so intimate a gesture. He glanced over his shoulder and saw that it was not her hand that was touching him, it was her body. She was leaning into him.

He jumped to his feet.

"Mr. Takamura," she said excitedly, "I'm sorry. It's just that your work has moved me very much." She took a step backward and reached up to her scarf, loosening the knot.

His heart was racing. Was she going to remove her scarf? Why had she touched him? His paltry English left him entirely. His palms began to sweat.

She gave a nervous laugh. "I was looking at the girl swinging toward him and then back and then toward him." She spoke rapidly. The foreign words glanced off him like darts. She let her scarf fall to the ground.

"It is a painting," he said weakly.

Her eyes were ablaze. "His eagerness . . . her terror . . ." The color had risen in her cheeks. Suddenly she grabbed his hand and pushed it under her skirt, pressing it to her wet crotch. He let out a small cry as he drew his hand away, then reached back to brace himself against the table. With horror, he realized that his sticky palm had left a large smudge on *Girl on a Swing.*

"Mr. Takamura, please."

"*Gomen kudasai, gomen kudasai,*" he mumbled. He piled *Girl on a Swing* on top of *Old Grandfather* on top of *School Children.* She was still babbling about sexual fantasies and art. He stuffed the pictures into the portfolio. Not bothering to zip it, he grabbed it and headed for the door, eyes straight ahead.

"Mr. Takamura?" she called out in a bewildered whisper.

The receptionist looked up as he bolted from the room.

Stephanie Waxman's fiction has appeared or is forthcoming in *The Bitter Oleander, The Distillery, Meridian, Oregon East* and *RE:AL*. She is also the author of *What Is a Girl? What Is a Boy?*, *Growing up Feeling Good* and *A Helping Handbook—When a Loved One Is Critically Ill.* She teaches in the UCLA Writers' Program and at Hebrew Union College.

A CAUTIONARY TELLING/*Naton Leslie*

MY FATHER IS A storyteller. He doesn't even know he is telling stories; he is simply talking, and what he has to say has a beginning, middle and end. It suits his temperament because he likes to be the center of attention. He often repeats the same stories—you could say he has a repertoire.

He is never overly theatrical when telling his stories because he is good at it. He knows all the right cues and markers, when to include dialogue and when to summarize, when to paint a scene or salt a detail. He seems to tell the story the same way each time, but if I could compare the latest telling with an earlier one, I am sure I would uncover refinements. I can see him at work, watching like a filmmaker at a screening for audience reactions to a rhythmic link or narrative aside. Part of his skill resides in his eyes. My father has a way of looking at you that is subtly coercive. It is actually a marriage of a look and a nod that says, "You know what I mean, of course. You know what I mean because you feel or think the same way and understand this part of the story because of its basic, undeniable truth." It is a tribal inclusion, and you find yourself nodding back, even if you aren't sure what pact you are signing with those eyes. This gives him the consent to continue the story—though an incomplete narrative is so compelling, so fetching, you'd agree with the devil to hear it out. "Go on," you are saying. "Finish the story. I'm with you."

I owe him a great debt of stories. Still, I can't retell them in conversation as he does because I don't have his authority of time and place. He once lived in the little mountain town of Clarion, Pennsylvania, where most of his stories are set; he grew up in Depression-era Appalachia, a time that forced people to make hard choices and bear the enormous weights of desperation and need. What the stories *mean* remains the only real collateral I can gather, but it is like trying to preserve soap bubbles. My father is not didactic and rarely reduces a story to a moral or a lesson; if pressed, I doubt he could say what a story is supposed to convey beyond its seamless events or its projection of character. They are only yarns. My father explains his need to tell stories this way: "There are three stages in a man's life: planning to do it; doing it; and talking about getting it done."

Here's a story he tells. Giles Philps grew up poor, what mountain folk call "growing up hard," down in Sligo, Pennsylvania, a borough to the south of Clarion, a place settled by Irish coal miners. They were what my father would call a rough breed, people who didn't think about much other than drinking, work and church and didn't make much of a distinction among the three. Such poverty has earned many metaphors to describe it, and in telling this story my father may employ one of them, saying Giles "didn't have two dimes to rub together" or, if he considers his poverty partially the result of shiftlessness or laziness, that he "didn't have a pot to piss in." Either way, such an upbringing marked Giles as prone to tragedy.

"Well," my father says, "Uncle Sam thought coal miners made good soldiers, so one day Giles got the letter saying, 'Your friends and neighbors have selected you to serve. . . .'" My father considers the euphemistic opening of a draft letter cynical—the one thing your friends and neighbors wouldn't do if they could help it is draft you headlong into a shooting war. But Giles went, with the sons of his friends and neighbors, into World War II, serving in Europe. Before he left he married "one of those pretty little Cramby girls from over in Oil City."

That's when my father shakes his head the way someone does when faced with something impossible to understand. This marriage was a moment of foreshadowing, and now we are to know that this will not last, that Melissa Cramby will figure into this tale in a larger, sad way. He may add that Giles "was a good-looking cuss," especially in uniform, to explain how she might make such a fatal mistake, or he may leave it there, relying on us knowing that lots of soldiers become husbands before going to war, leaving behind counties full of widows.

At the war's end Giles came back with a uniform festooned with decorations, and he and Melissa bought a little house in a hollow down by the trout stream they call Gravel Lick, a creek now ruined by mine runoff and probably already candied with sulfur by then, as the mines were going full bore. That's where Giles found a job as a shooter, or dynamiter.

He and Melissa had four boys, and up until now there is really no story, but my father understands the value of background and setting and certainly dispatches this picture with broad brushes. Then comes the change agent. A normal life, at least one normal for mountain folk, is a setup for something to intercede. This element is usually avoidable and leads you to believe his story has a moral, that it's a simple example of what this or that will get you. It could be you in this story, he suggests for a moment. This pricks his listener's ear, not only because you can see another story evolving but also because the listener is implicated, has been singled out for learning. You are involved because maybe this is your life too if you don't pay attention. Listen up. This part is important.

Giles began to drink. There it is, the finger of change, the nudge of disaster. Everyone likes a drink, and you'd find lots of strip miners down at the Sigel Hotel after their shifts, washing back coal dust and replacing the howling and grinding of heavy machinery with the slippery tones of the steel guitar and the plaintive gravel of Hank Snow, a combination that made you slump your shoulders over your beer, replacing weariness with blues and loss. Then you could go home, a little light-headed but ready for supper.

However, when my father says someone "began to drink," he means someone has taken it up as a serious enterprise. Soon he'd be the last of the miners to leave, and once at home with Melissa would, as my father says, "treat her mean," which can translate into anything from vicious argument to violence and need not be explicated because such horrors are unspeakable. Here he pauses to shake his head again, since Giles is "making his own bed" of sorrow and regret and later will lie in it. "Well," he says, "they kept fighting, and before long they separated."

After that Giles really started going downhill. He kept drinking; you could find him any late night down at the Blue Goose, where the earlier crowd had left a residue of riff-raff, like Snubs Gray and Carny Charles, minor characters who often show up in my father's stories. Snubs, for instance, got his nickname for his habit of picking up snubbed-out and smoldering cigarettes on the street and puffing them back to life. He and Carny also appear in a story about the day a truck loaded with liquor didn't quite negotiate the River Hill and missed the bridge over the Clarion River. In that story, Snubs, Carny and a squadron of town drunks line up on the bridge, diving into the river to salvage floating crates of booze.

No good could come from the company of these men, and Giles "got bad." He lost his job as a shooter because you needed a steady hand, and the boss gave him a job as an oiler, a maintenance position that paid less. He moved into an old tool shack on an abandoned mine site.

One Saturday morning he drove into town. He parked in front of the police station, walked in, marched up to the chief of police's desk and said, "Well, I'm turning myself in. I killed Snubs Gray."

"What's that you said?" the chiefasked.

"I killed Snubs last night," he repeated, standing straight and still.

"Ah, come on, Giles, you sure?"

"Oh, he's dead all right. I've seen plenty of dead men. We were drinking last night and got to fighting, and I hit him with a chair—I know that much—but I don't know what all else I might have done to him." Here my father reports that Giles was "as calm as you please," which means he was either coldly murderous or unflinchingly courageous—he leaves the interpretation up to you, dangling a bit of ambiguity.

"Let's go see," the chief said. "Let's get in my car, and we'll go down to the mine." The police chief was probably Joe Strolpe, who gets named in other stories when he is the butt of a prank, such as the time my father and Marv Johnson hacksawed the parking meters off on Main Street in Clarion and left them inside Strolpe's car. But when he is taking a measured, just action or an admirable one, he remains nameless, uncredited. My father holds some unrevealed grudge against him and always finds a way to repay some perceived slight or offense.

When they got there, the chief walked in with Giles right behind him. There was Snubs, lying on the floor. Dead. The one-room shack was filthy: a floor fouled with spilled beer, a broken-down bed reeking of sweat, with very little furniture besides it and a littered table and two chairs. The air stank so badly the chief had to hold his breath. Giles had been living like an animal.

The chief went back outside, Giles listlessly following him, and after Giles was safely locked in the back of the car—in case he had second thoughts and decided to make a run for it across the ruined hills and sour ponds of the strip mine—the chief called for an ambulance to get the body. Then he went back inside the shack, as much as he wished he didn't have to, to describe the scene for his report. There, he described Snubs's wounds on a tablet, and as he looked around the shack he saw something that surprised him. On a nail across the room hung a full-dress army uniform, the jacket, shirt and trousers neatly pressed and spotless and on a hanger, a beret cocked on the nail above. He walked over and pulled open the coat flap; the shirt was covered in military medals and bars, what they call "salad." Looking down, he saw a pair of combat boots standing heels together below the uniform, polished and ready for inspection.

Strolpe had avoided the draft in World War II by declaring he was an only son—I only know this from another story my father tells. In this story, though, that is left out. What is important is that the uniform gave the chief an idea. He locked Giles in the jailhouse and over the course of a weekend found out who had been Giles's commanding officer in the war.

It was going to be a short trial, but an army colonel Strolpe had called managed to show up before it was over to testify on Giles's behalf. This part of the story is summarized quickly, compressed into a few facts. Giles, the officer said, had been an army Ranger, a member of an elite commando corps trained for behind-the-lines and hand-to-hand fighting. However, the reason Giles came back heavily decorated was that he had gone above and beyond the call of duty even for a Ranger. The government had not publicized his deeds because much of what he had done was still classified, but, the colonel said gravely, "Giles Philps saw some jagged, terrible parts of the war."

Giles did not react but sat in his chair stiffly, as square-shouldered as the day he had turned himself in; he had grimly saluted the colonel when he entered the courtroom, and the officer had returned the gesture. The judge could see in Giles the outline of the young man who had been yanked out of Sligo, Pennsylvania, and had been asked to do things no one should be asked to do and had done them unflinchingly and well. Today we have a set of clinical definitions for Giles Philps's problems, but my father said he did not seem to have what was then called "shell shock." He had been left to fend for himself upon returning from war, to dislodge whatever horrors he bore however he could. He had lost that fight.

The judge took his military record into consideration in the sentencing, though, and Giles went to prison for manslaughter, not murder, and served seven years of a fifteen-year sentence. When he came back to town, he was never the same again. He was sober and clean, but on most days could be found in the park across from the Clarion County courthouse, on a bench near the Civil War memorial. He was always well dressed, in a crisp fedora, jacket and tie, and usually sat there, sweetly silent, staring at some spot across town.

The town would have allowed Giles to be forgotten, a whispered presence in the park, had he simply sat there. However, whenever someone passed his bench on the sidewalk he would rise to his feet, remove his hat and press it to his chest and say softly, "Good evening, Melissa," no matter what time of day it happened to be. He was playing the part of the young miner, scrubbed up and starched straight, courting his long-ago wife. I guess for Giles it was always evening.

But that's not the end of the story, of course. Though it seems Giles has reached his end, a muddled state from which he will never reemerge, this much has all been a setup, you realize, if you have listened to enough of my father's stories. What comes next is not an epilogue, nor is it a topper—an extension of the story's culmination for another beat or two. The rest is the real story, the moment he has been meaning to get to, the act of grace or meaning with a permanent pregnancy.

"One day," my father continues, Giles heard that one of his sons had gotten drunk and then into some sort of trouble with one of the college girls. "Some sort of trouble" can mean some terrible things, especially when combined with drink, but my father leaves it to your imagination because he doesn't want to get sidetracked down another crooked path of wrongdoing: this is Giles Philps's story, not his son's. What's more, my father wants the son's offense to remain nameless so we don't turn against him. The son should remain salvageable, so we are led away from his transgressions with what happened next.

Giles left his position in the park and went to Melissa's house down on Gravel Lick, where the boy was living, walking the whole way. Though it was several miles, he arrived without so much as a hitch in his step, fairly leapt onto the porch, banged the screen door open and charged into the house. He found his son in the kitchen.

The son stood, staring wide-eyed at the man who had just walked into his life, a man who hadn't said "Boo" to him for years. That's when Giles "grabbed about two handfuls of him" and threw him up against the kitchen counter.

"What are you trying to do, you stupid son of a bitch?" Giles said. "Look in the mirror." He bent the boy backward over the counter and thrust his face inches from his. "Look at me. I'm a goddamn mirror."

Now my father stops, giving his trademark narrow-eyed look of knowing, and then he barely nods, sealing the tale and the transaction. You understand, the look says, you know what this is all about; that's why I told you—because I realized you'd understand. You have bought into the tale, his lingering gaze contends, and you are banking the story for future reference, for the collateral of meaning that will rise from it again and again. You have been given this story because you are someone who understands the sublime lessons to be learned in such things, feeling such stories in the hollow of your chest, in the base of your skull, where it registers in the short hairs, in the skin of the back and arms.

In truth my father does not have a secure sense of what this story means, or what any of his stories mean. He merely tells them, and senses such tales have their own resonances; they must be told, or why else should someone like Giles suffer, and why else would my father remember his suffering and be able to recall it with such exquisite detail? Perhaps, though, the story has accrued these meanings in the glacial way most stories acquire their urgency. The story has taken up residence in his mind for a reason, he is sure, and telling it gives it the life it demands and transmits it with a viral quickness and surety. Giles is left there, in the kitchen of a little country house along the ruined Gravel Lick, his son bent back in terror. If the son is lucky, his father has given him a glimpse into the future, and he will see it fully and change his ways. If Giles is lucky, he has made something out of the scrap heap of what he has seen and done. Telling it makes it so. Or increases the likelihood.

"Imagine," my father said the last time he told Giles's story, "imagine having no kind of pride in yourself except in something you've already done and can't do again. That's what gets to me." There were plenty of things in Giles's past that he couldn't repeat: drinking, murder and war. I'm not sure which of these my father was pointing to, perhaps all of them, but that was what the story meant, at least that time it was told.

Naton Leslie's essays have appeared in *The North American Review, Fourth Genre, High Plains Literary Review, Mid-American Review* and other magazines. In 2003 a collection of his short fiction, *Marconi's Dream and Other Stories,* was published by The Texas Review Press as the George Garrett Fiction Prize winner; he was also awarded a fellowship in literary nonfiction from the New York Foundation for the Arts.

ISLAMADORA/*Lissa Franz*

THE WOMEN OF THE OFFICE gather around Pilar's desk to play Who Has the Worst Children. The higher up they are in the office hierarchy, the more offensive and shocking their offspring. Allison, Pilar's boss and the CFO of the company, has four-year-old twin boys who dump Hershey's syrup on the couch and call each other "shit-head." Janet, in-house legal counsel, has three moody girls, six, eight and ten, who torment their bus driver and are up all night with lucid dreams. May, from accounting, has a twelve-year-old son who recently became a vegetarian and won't even eat chicken broth when it is baked into things.

Pilar is the secretary. Her job requires knowing whose child is calling when a teary voice says, "Can I talk to my mom," sorting the mail and ordering supplies. Her daughter, Thea, is sixteen. She is six foot two and plays the flute with a timidity that makes people look away while she performs.

Pilar's office mates fawn over Thea when she visits the office. They have a lurid fascination with Pilar, who had her daughter at eighteen, the age when they were applying to colleges and weighing things like "best party school" against "lowest teacher-student ratio." Pilar is their link to a world where people clean their own houses and don't have college degrees and live in rentals that back up to the highway. The women in the office call her "honey" or, if they are very high up like Allison, "love." *Could you get that for me, love?* The men in the office call her Pilar and glance at their watches while speaking to her.

The women don't allow Pilar to participate in Who Has the Worst Children. Whenever she moves to speak, they pat her on the back and tell her that Thea is perfect. Pilar allows the implicit condescension because she enjoys having the women gather spontaneously around her desk in the middle of the day; she lures them with industrial-sized tubs of cheap chocolate. These women wear black suits and Chanel shoes; they attended Yale and Northwestern. She loves to hear their problems with their lawn services and their summer houses. They stress that Pilar's life has just followed a different path, as if her life is an entity they have separated from Pilar herself. They make a big show with their flattery. "We don't know how you did it, honey. Imagine having a baby at *eighteen!* God, I was cracking up my father's cars one by one, the big ones and then the little ones." This was Allison, who went to Harvard. In these women's lives Harvard/Yale/Northwestern is where you go to get some education and jump-start the all-important networking that will stay with you for the rest of your life. It is not where you meet a husband; you meet the husband much later on, post–graduate school and the first job, where you work eighty-hour weeks. These women find love when they are at the pinnacle of their exhaustion, in their early thirties, and are beginning to feel some need for a biological diversion.

If Pilar were allowed to play, this is the winning worst-child story she would like to tell: yesterday she caught Thea having sex with her boyfriend, Robbie, a senior planning to be a theater major at NYU in the fall. She caught them in Thea's bed making small, restrained burps of noise, sandwiched and rolling. With great deliberation Pilar went back outside, reentered the house and spent some time banging around the kitchen, in part to relieve her anger. They had often discussed how Thea would go on the pill if she was contemplating sex, and Pilar had assumed her own lighthearted permissiveness would lead her daughter to be level-headed and responsible.

"We didn't expect you back so soon, Mrs. Kenning," Rob had joked when they arrived in the kitchen, insinuating a mature relationship with his levity. Usually he was deathly serious, and for the first time Pilar pictured him at NYU—him and his big act.

If Pilar told this story to the women of the office, they would focus on the sex. That was the difference between them and Pilar. Pilar didn't give a shit about whether or not her daughter was having sex; this was not the issue. Sex was going to happen, and Pilar knew that better than anyone. It happened, most likely, when you were ready for it to happen, unless you were unlucky or unwise. Thea was neither of these. There was the brisk evidence: Thea had been on top of Robbie, in her own bed. It was not the position of someone doing something against her will.

The issue, to Pilar, was not the cute story about catching her daughter in the sack with her boyfriend. Rather, it was the fear that Thea would somehow manage to lead a life exactly like Pilar's.

A woman slips into the office at 11:45, wearing a drapey pantsuit and the pointy heels that women of a certain age stuff their feet into with some ill-conceived vanity. She is recovering from a tan that was only pretty when deep and new.

She sidles up to Pilar's formidable desk, clutching her bag.

"Hello? So sorry to disturb you at your work. I'm Anita. Robbie's mother?"

At Anita's insistence they walk to the fancy hotel restaurant, the kind with miles of empty oak tables and bulbous water glasses and a draft problem. Pilar looks at her watch to remind Robbie's mother that she's on her lunch hour. She suspects Anita would love to pickle over a two-hour lunch.

Hidden behind the tall, leatherette menu, Anita says, "I'm concerned about the relationship between Thea and Robbie. It's getting very intense, and he's losing some of his focus on school. And then there's the spring play. He has to find time to learn all of those lines. I've spoken to Robbie. Could you speak to Thea? I know they go to your house, Pilar, and I know you aren't home." She comes out from behind the menu to take a sip of her Pellegrino. "Thea really is a *darling* girl. I've enjoyed getting to know her. And to hear her play the flute!"

"Oh, she practices all the time," Pilar says, smiling. Thea is a mediocre flautist and practices—with flabby rumbles and high, screeching inaccuracies—only when something is troubling her. "I'll talk to her, but I'm not going to tell her to stop seeing Robbie. Honestly, it'll just make them like each other more. You remember how that goes."

"You seem like you've already given up, Pilar." Contempt rims Anita's voice. "I'm not willing to let it go so easily. Or maybe—" she brightens up here at the thought—"you just don't see it."

"What don't I see?"

"The enormous amount they have to lose," Anita says.

Pilar rips at her crusty bun and tries not to laugh.

Anita says, "How old are you, Pilar?"

"What are you getting at?"

"I'm just curious." Anita laughs daintily, a little sprig of a laugh carefully placed to ease the tension. "It's tough navigating this, isn't it? Not to be too heavy-handed, not to seem like we're trying to live their lives, catch every mistake before they make it?"

Could they have this entire conversation without discussing sex? Pilar wonders. Finally she says, "Kids have sex, Anita. They have the desire, the ache, the need, and an overabundance of time and cunning. Perhaps you have forgotten. I guess I haven't. I haven't forgotten at all."

Anita pushes away an arrangement of baby greens squirted with lemon, which she has only picked at. "I didn't have a boyfriend until college," she says primly. She is easily fifty-two years old. "Even then I took things slowly. I can't stand around and watch him throw everything away. I'm sorry if you think I'm too old-fashioned. It's what I think. How I feel." She dabs her lips with a napkin still preserved in the shape of a duck.

At Thea's age, Pilar was pregnant, sitting hot-cheeked with her mother at the OB's office, trying to ignore the perky magazine articles in the waiting room: "Keep the Romance after Baby!" She gave up school; years later she spent three months studying for the GED and just barely passed. Without the pace of classes and the airless cafeteria and the sudden grass smell in the halls in spring, the information seemed impossible to absorb. Gone was her eagerness to ascend a ladder of knowledge that would actually lead somewhere. Yet she did not think, then or now, that she had ruined her life. That other women—the ones who controlled their lives with a dumb, schooled, strict precision—considered it a ruined life was her cross to bear.

Her entrée arrives, a slab of salmon she cannot afford. Pilar removes the spiral spine and feathery bones with her fingers and eats them. Of course Anita relishes her son's entanglement; it gives her purpose before she loses control of him for good. Anita stirs and stirs her bisque, then looks up apologetically.

"Too hot," she says.

That night Pilar leans on Thea's doorjamb. It's eleven, and Thea is up studying for a Biology exam. Her flute is on her bed, a damp circle on her bedspread beneath the mouthpiece.

Pilar says, "I had lunch with Robbie's mother today."

Thea's eyes flutter with alarm.

"She's worried you're getting too serious."

Thea juts her shoulders back. "It wouldn't matter, if I were a different kind of girl."

"What kind of girl is that?"

Thea blushes scarlet. "The kind you can slice open and find some sort of certificate of perfection."

Pilar cocks her head.

"You know what I'm saying, Mom. She likes connections. You can see that. She wants Robbie to *marry well*." At the word *marry* her face flushes scarlet all over again. "He called me already and told me what she said. I don't need to hear it twice. She thinks we're going to run away and get married."

"Well?"

"Well what?" Thea says. She sits up straight and yawns. She spends her best studying hours with Robbie, then stays up all night with schoolwork. "I'm not getting married, Mom, and you know it. I'm sixteen, for God's sake."

"I'd know if you were getting married."

"Yes," Thea says. "Yes, you probably would. It's not even *legal*."

Pilar nods. Thea's father, who lent Thea her height—and a brittle-ness of spirit, as if someone is constantly shining a flashlight in her eyes and demanding to know what she thinks—was just old enough to ask her, but instead he took a train to Florida and started a new life. He is not a shit, as everyone assumes; he does not miss his child-sup-port payments. He is a third grade teacher in a progressive elementary school, married to a bohemian woman named Fin who gave him two lovely, big-boned daughters.

"Let me tell you what happens when you have a baby this young." Pilar studies Thea's face. "Ten years later, when the dust clears, you start to yearn for respectability. Maybe it's the fact that no one has respected you since you had the baby. People say dumb, hurtful things about your age in the supermarket line. Sometimes in order to avoid this you pretend to be the babysitter. Reality dictates that you can't go to college, not a four-year, expensive, live-in-a-dorm-and-drink-till-you-puke college, anyway; so you don't go at all; community college is beneath you. None of the jobs you get make any money, but they are decent. You test hospital equipment, manage retail stores and do the whole world's clerical work. Some women, of course, take the high road and kill themselves to go through college one class at a time. They become lawyers." Pilar loves to despise these women who sit on school boards and volunteer profusely and grin too loosely for women with so much schooling, overcome by where their anger at the world has taken them. Pilar is not one of them. She does not burn up all the time. At night she sews, which is a grand substitute for a Torts class. "You may not think you care about being respected. That's what being a teenager is all about. You push all the buttons, and your parents are embarrassing nags, and you love to do the wrong thing. You love that you don't crave respect, that it means nothing to you. I'm just warning you, honey. Just—be careful."

Thea sighs. "I hear you, Mom."

Pilar can count on one hand how many times she has repeated this advice, so the sigh, with its implication that Pilar is nagging, makes her furious. "I want you on the pill. Now. End of discussion."

Thea doesn't look up, but pretends to be absorbed in a page entitled MAMMALS, with sketches of the unlikely members of that class: whales, bats, platypuses. Pilar's mind flashes back to nursing her daughter in her childhood bedroom, her parents next door. She was desperate to leave; she was an adult with a baby. She can't picture Thea doing the same thing; Thea is a *child*.

"Fine," the child says.

"I'll make you an appointment with my gynecologist."

"You have to come with me," she says, fighting tears.

On the bed, Thea is an amalgam of all their battles: thick eyeliner, a scooped-out shirt that shows a black bra strap and the padded push-ups that fill her out, skin-tight yoga pants rolled down twice to expose the pointy points of her hips. Pilar sees how much she looks like every one of the friends she brings home: a sort of sloppy, thin, fuzzy-armed, unassuming girl with an unmistakable air of sex, though not sluttish-ness: the doe-eyed, unassuming kind specifically designed to make their mothers pay attention.

"My advice," Pilar says, ignoring Thea's tears, "is to cool it with Robbie for just a little while. Give each other some space. Don't cut it off, but just relax. He's not going anywhere yet. You've got all spring and then all summer."

Thea stops sniveling and leans down on her arm. Pilar can tell she would love to reveal the acuteness of what she is feeling, but can't. It's over between them, the little-girl trust and shy love. Pilar is one tough thirty-four-year-old who makes her own clothes and doesn't trim her hair and manages to wear secretary clothes—vests, clogs, cute pins—to the office without really trying. On bad nights, lonely nights, Pilar dreams up some version of a makeover, complete with short, funky hair and black clothes, but this is more a fantasy of escape than a real desire to change. She would never want Thea to believe that she's thought about trading in her life.

Pilar deposits a sleepy, muted Thea at school the next morning and walks into the bakery next to her office. Carl fumbles his way to the front, red envelopes beneath his eyes from being up all night, and again Pilar regrets sleeping with him. His house was irresistible: a ranch sur-rounded on four sides by farm fields. She was seduced by the silence; her own house, a stucco rental seated by the exit ramp of the highway, is permeated with the relentless, animal drone of traffic. There is a chainlink fence behind it that collects all manner of things people lose from their cars: sneakers, money, novels, lamps, lumber, greasy French-fry sacks. She has lived in this house for fourteen years, hooked on the low maintenance, the cheap rent and—somehow—its depressing view. There is something addictive about not caring.

Carl ties on a clean apron as she makes her way up in the line, and she asks for coffee and a chocolate brioche she knows he made him-self.

"Hi, sweetheart," Carl says, shyly. He said "I love you" on their third date. That was the night she slept with him.

"Hi, Carl," Pilar says. She takes her coffee as everyone watches them. Carl only comes to the front for her.

"How are things? Thea?"

"Fine, everything's fine." Pilar hands him the exact, memorized amount, and smiles. "We ought to get together."

Carl's eyes light up. "Yes, yes. I'll call you."

"Okay," Pilar says, with dread. "See you later."

She walks to her office, settles in at her desk. She reads her e-mail and answers the phone and says good morning to the late arrivals, usually the dads with small children. Dave, the UPS man, comes in, and she flirts with him as he dashes about in his tight brown uniform. Then Allison comes out and plunks herself down on Pilar's huge desk, a clearance area for office mail and packages and plants people don't want anymore and all the bits of memo paper, some of them skewered on a metal spindle. Allison has finished the seven-minute nap she commences with every morning, which she calls "the real person's yoga." She is wearing a suit with a skirt instead of trousers and everything is taupe-colored, even her heels. Her hair has recently been highlighted, and Pilar loves the little-girl stripes of pure blond.

Allison peels the wrapper off a Mr. Goodbar.

"Alec and Sam are driving me crazy," she says. "Really, Pilar, I don't think I'm cut out for this sometimes. I'm forty-*four*, for God's sake. I'm starting to feel sorry for the au pair. Do you think we are too lenient with the boys?"

Pilar thinks of the gym and music classes, the swimming lessons, the early-intervention speech therapy, the miniature-rodeo birthday parties, the designer clothes and French tutors.

"I don't think so," Pilar says.

Janet walks by. "The girls were up all night," she says. "They heard something. We all heard it, actually; I think it was a wild cat—and then they wouldn't go back to sleep. We all ended up in the kitchen at two A.M. One little disruption and wham! Everyone's hungry, my husband is down in the kitchen making pancakes."

May arrives holding sheets of numbers, which at a distance look like landscapes.

Janet continues, "The whole house is clean, it's silent, and the girls sit at the kitchen table with this sweet zombie look. We light candles, and we talk. What can get better than that? It does not, however, fit into a paradigm of quality family time. Or maybe it is really some kind of fucked-up version of family time. The ultimate family time. We sit around thinking we're getting away with something. Nobody has to get in the car, I'm not complaining about grocery shopping,

Mike's not late for work. It's not Saturday, the day we make depressing lists of things that have to get done, nor is it Sunday, when we all get those nudgy headaches because we're overtired and we've stopped moving."

"You're enabling the behavior," Pilar says. "Shame on you."

May says, "I think you've found one of those alternative universes."

Allison chews thoughtfully on what must be her last chocolate. Pilar wants the conversation to go on and on, but the other women are smoothing their silks and sighing.

"Right in your very own house," Allison says finally, balling up her collection of wrappers and aiming for the can. "How exquisite."

Sean, Thea's father, calls that night while Pilar is pinning Thea a rose-colored linen tank top for summer. It is February, and this gives her something to look forward to, combing the bolts of linens with their sharp, chemical smells, seeing if the shadow of her hand disappears or not behind different fabrics—is this one too sheer?—studying the coarse criss-cross of the fibers and their heft.

Sean says, "Could I speak with Thea?" He is always polite, and he never asks after Pilar. He reminds her of the men in her office, who seem strangely devoid of personality. She knows Sean still has one, or he wouldn't always win Teacher of the Year. When he went to Florida she loosely followed his phases: garage band, Outward Bound instructor, a brief move to Miami Beach and an even briefer stint as a physical therapist, until he went back to school for his teaching degree and moved to Pensacola. She was shocked when he got married, right on time, and had two daughters. She, too, never asked about him or his life, until one time Thea came home from a two-week vacation with him when she was eleven and exploded: "I can't believe you never ask about him, that you could just care less about whether or not he is happy!" Pilar had said, "Okay. Well? Is he happy? Is he *happy*?" and Thea had looked at her with wide eyes and burst into tears. "Yes, Mommy. I guess so."

As she goes to get Thea, Pilar listens to Sean breathe, her hand clamped over the mouthpiece. It reminds her of how he used to whisper when they discussed their plans. He would plant his mouth in her ear. She never did sleep all night in bed with him, entwined. Their sex was unmemorable and urgent. Her first thought when she realized she was pregnant and would have the baby was that she would never lose him.

"Hey, sweets," Sean says to Thea. Pilar hears how his voice crackles and comes back alive, and they discuss her forthcoming trip to Florida.

Before the advent of February vacation Thea begins to enjoy the torturous separation from Robbie. She tries out the gully of despair and decides, Pilar sees, that it is dark and alluring. Pilar is glad to see her go to Florida, still slow-moving, sighing too much and obsessed with the phone. She has begun running after school, a loping and frowning mile or two, and Pilar is tired of begging her to eat. Let Sean and Fin coax her out of her own head. She kisses Thea good-bye at Logan and navigates the labyrinth of construction that has become Boston, stopping for a few hours to buy fabric along a disconnected street behind Downtown Crossing.

She arrives home just as Thea's plane should be touching down and finds Robbie on her front step. He wears the cargo pants all the skinny boys wear that make them look skinnier, and his face is blotchy, as if he's been crying.

"Thea's in Florida," Pilar says in greeting. She tries to be polite, but she is mad at him for launching Thea into heartbreak and then showing up the second she is gone. It stinks of cowardice and immaturity, and Pilar does not want to talk to him right now.

"Lucky her." Robbie peeks into Pilar's bag: a geometric silk and an unusual hempy linen, spools of thread, papery interfacing. "Cool."

"I could make you something, Robbie. We could get you into something other than cargo pants."

"Cool." He hitches up his pants protectively.

"What can I do for you?" Robbie follows her into the kitchen, where Pilar sheds her coat and longs for a quiet house. There are five phone messages, and she knows they are from Carl. He leaves messages like a train wreck, calling again and again, adding and subtracting.

"It's just—I have to learn my lines. I have to know them by Monday, and Thea was supposed to help me. I mean—I wanted her to help me, and she left. I just thought if I came over here—" He forces a laugh. "Maybe just standing in this kitchen."

Pilar doesn't return his anxious grin; she crosses her arms. "She waited for you to call for two weeks. You didn't call. You didn't ask her for help. She would have gladly helped."

"I'm leaving in the fall," Robbie blurts out. His face blotches with the effort of holding himself in. "It's over."

Now Pilar laughs. "It's a bit calculated, don't you think, Robbie? Life doesn't have to be cruel like that." He starts gulping for air, and still Pilar doesn't offer to read through his lines with him.

Instead, she watches him drive away while picturing Thea in Sean's makeshift guest room. Thea hangs her clothes in a little armoire filled with the detritus of Sean's legitimate daughters: adorable Halloween costumes, bits of holiday wrapping paper, matching dresses long outgrown. Thea pushes it all aside, stoic with the effort of being her father's first daughter.

"They're fighting a lot," whispers Thea. "It's bumming me out."

Pilar coaches her daughter a little, listening to her tell about her half-sister Monica's Zoloft and Fin's inability to spend any time at the dinner table.

"You know what, Mom," Thea says. "I don't really care how screwed up they are. They're not *mine*. But it sucks to be here right now. I want to come home."

"Put your father on," Pilar says.

"Hi," Sean says. "What?"

"Thea should come home."

"What do you mean? We're having a great time. She's just missing her boyfriend."

"She wants to change her flight."

Silence. "No way. She's just a little homesick. What would she do at home? I've been taking her to the beach. We've been miniature golfing. She's just a little quiet, is all. Leave her be. She can mope anywhere."

Pilar says, "She's enjoying the moping."

Sean laughs. "Oh, yes."

Her heart thunks along its corridors for a man she doesn't know, for the way he used to gently handle his books, for the cheap cologne, *Homme,* he sprayed onto his collars. His voice has an older edge to it, a teacherly superiority that it didn't have when he visited her at home, holding colicky Thea away from his body in fright.

"I don't mind either way. But if she's unhappy . . ."

"She's fine," Sean says.

By midweek Pilar starts to act like she's on vacation. She doesn't clean; she doesn't cook; she puts off Carl until the weekend and sews an impractical shoulder bag for Thea with the linen and lined with the silk; it's beautiful, and she sews in the box top of Thea's favorite cereal to give the bottom a hint of shape. She still goes in to work but does very little except answer the phones. On her lunch breaks she looks at houses, entering into a politely thrilling relationship with a broker, Nicole, who wears elegant black clothes and drives her around in a mint-infused Volvo.

On Friday night she makes dinner for Carl. She should be nervous because he is an excellent cook, but for some reason—because she doesn't love him, because he is overweight and too jolly and tries always to say the right thing—she doesn't really care how the food is and drinks too much wine. They fall into a predictable schedule, in a heap on her bed by nine-thirty after a go at a terrible rental film he thought would be good and wasn't.

In the morning Pilar cooks again, this time with love because she adores breakfast: the lingering over coffee with her matted hair and second helpings of granola and yogurt and chocolate brioche. Carl leaves around noon. It is with some confusion that Pilar, on her last free day without Thea, realizes she really wants to go into the office to check on a few things she'd been neglecting all week, to feel the cool animal HVAC system asleep in the ceiling and to sit in the dark.

She isn't there three minutes when Allison comes slamming through the door. She immediately whacks all the lights on, and Pilar sees she is wearing high-tech sneakers, a ponytail and skin-tight sweats. She wears no makeup, and because of this her face appears smaller, ashy and young. She sees Pilar and stops dead.

"Oh, hi, love," she says. "Just coming in to decompress."

She has told Pilar that on occasion she comes to work on the weekends to escape the boys, but Pilar always assumed she was joking.

Allison says, "What are you doing here?"

"Oh, I had some things to catch up with. Thea went to Florida to see Sean."

"Sean?"

"Her father."

"Thea's *father?* Here." She slides onto Pilar's desk and unwraps a Kit Kat.

"You look like you're the one in need," Pilar says, chewing.

Allison laughs. "I'm hiding. Really. The beasts. I miss them all week, I feel guilty all goddamn week, and then on the weekends I hate them. Really. I hate my own children." She laughs. "Tell me sixteen is easier."

"Exactly the same behavior," Pilar says. "Only they're smarter than you."

Allison takes a Special Dark and stares. "So. What's he like?"

Pilar thinks of walking to Thea's room, holding Sean's voice in her hand. She says, "I'm still in love with him."

"What?" Allison squints. "You've got to be kidding. What happened?" She looks at Pilar with a different focus than she would during a workday, and it makes Pilar want to confess.

"When Thea was three months old he disappeared. About four days later—I was frantic with wondering where he'd gone—he ended up in some seedy little bar in the Florida Keys that's basically a shrine to the Hurricane of 1935. Hundreds of people were swept out to sea, whole families lost. A brand-new railroad was being built, in part to employ veterans during the Depression. So a train was sent, and of course it pulled in to Islamadora—I can still remember the exotic way this sounded, the way Sean pronounced it—and all these people boarded, only to be hit by a wall of water. I guess that was the end of the railroad. It was the middle of the night when he called; I was breastfeeding Thea in my childhood bedroom. I couldn't picture the Keys, I'd never even been to Florida. I said to him, *But what about us, Sean? What about me and Thea?* I've never heard anyone cry like he did then, when I asked him that." Pilar trails off, thinking of Robbie standing in her kitchen and the steely way she reacted to his hysterics. "Sean never came back."

It was all clear to her now: until setting foot in that bar, Sean had thought of his leaving as an act of courage. Then he realized he was no different than all those dead men shunted out to sea. He had no intention of being a husband or father, and he was never going back. Pilar thinks of the years it took to come to this realization herself; it is not a stretch of her life she wants to relive. "I call him the Grief Train. Like, the Grief Train's on the phone! He's been great to Thea, somehow; he always calls her and wants to be involved. After he settled down with his new wife, anyway."

Allison nods, absorbed. "And you've never been married? Don't tell me you've been secretly waiting around for this guy. All this time? You're so . . ." Allison pauses, and Pilar holds her breath.

"Accessible. And pretty. Pretty and accessible."

Pilar is not pretty. She's elegant when she wants to be, when dressed for something formal and inspiring. "Pretty" is daily and fresh; Pilar is dark, and her look is full of storms. "Accessible"? It makes Pilar think of a snack machine. In goes the coin, out the bag of chips!

"I just haven't found anyone who doesn't make me feel self-conscious. I'm very self-conscious all the time. When you are in love you feel invisible. You are absorbed instead of studied. I haven't found that again. I guess I'm still looking." She's babbling; the office feels strange on a Saturday. She feels strange.

Allison leans over and puts her arms around Pilar. It is awkward, and Pilar finds herself only able to see the floor.

"I'm happy you've felt that kind of love. Really, I am, Pilar. But that kind of love—the absorbing, cloud-nine kind—is only perfect for teenagers. The rest of the time things are not so perfect. There are roadblocks. You must meet in the middle as two separate people. And nobody,

nobody disappears."

Pilar opens her mouth to defend herself, and can't. Sharp tears, with water that hurts, spring into her eyes. It isn't that she expected it to be easy; it isn't that she wants to be saved. It's impossible to explain this to Allison. "Stop thinking this guy is going to come back," Allison continues, oblivious, her Harvard tones coming through. She gives Pilar's shoulders one last squeeze and jumps off the desk. She isn't an athletic woman, only the kind who would sign up for a trendy class and not sweat very much. "Pilar, I don't mean to hurt you, but you need to get on with your life."

Pilar drives back into Boston on Sunday morning and sits at Logan, near the luggage carrels, where massive black duffel bags rotate around the belt far ahead of the passengers. Thea arrives nearly last, trudging, but when she sees Pilar her face changes dramatically. She smiles in relief, as if at the end of an ordeal, and Pilar feels guilty. She lopes toward Pilar, wearing sneakers and nylon track pants—something she has on must always make noise—and a sleek pink shirt, something new. Her long hair is French braided in a crooked and puckered way, obviously by her young half-sisters. When she reaches Pilar she hugs her tightly, taking great long sighs. They collect Thea's bag off the carrel and walk, close together, to the car.

Pilar loves the way her daughter talks on the way home, loose and relaxed, about it all: Fin's crying jags, the orange trees and roseated spoonbills, her stress zit, Sean's Spanish curse words, Julie's Barbie collection.

They have been home ten minutes when Robbie shows up. It makes Pilar sad to see Thea close herself up to impress him. At dinner Pilar gives them some tasks so she can enjoy watching them play, bumping into each other and brushing hands and tossing their heads, a game of silent charades, seeing how much they can communicate without talking.

After dinner they watch a TV movie until Thea realizes she has three chapters to read for U.S. History. Robbie wraps his arms around Thea by the door and whispers in her ear, and he holds her for a long time, rubbing his hand on the small of her back and between her shoulder blades.

When he is gone Pilar does a hem, something that needs all of her attention to be straight, and when she is finished she stops by Thea's room. Thea is sprawled on her bed, reading.

"I'm sorry it was a hard trip," Pilar says.

Thea answers right away. It's obvious she has not been working on her history. "Dad always tries too hard to win me. As if there is nothing in between. He always wants to start over. It's very tiring. But maybe it's a little bit my fault, too. Maybe I'm just not what he expects."

Pilar nods, though she has no idea what Thea means. Sean left behind this girl who looks and acts exactly like him. Even her mannerism now, of cocking her head to think, looks like him. How could he not understand her perfectly?

Pilar says, "You're a good girl, Thea."

Thea looks up, puzzled. "No, Mom," she says, laughing softly, "I'm not."

Pilar's heart floods with the realization that she still knows more than her daughter, and for this reason Thea still needs her, perhaps will always need her. Pilar is out in front. "I think you're good. I think you're great, and the best, and I'm lucky to have you."

Thea sighs and forces a sad smile. "I know you do, Mom. Thanks."

Somewhere toward two A.M., Pilar has to use the bathroom. She pads in and out and is about to climb back into bed when she hears something strange. Some small rustling, a strange, delicate whine.

Pilar automatically bolts over to Thea's room. She hesitates and listens. Then she knows: it is Robbie.

Pilar goes back to her room, wondering if Robbie will be there in the morning. She doubts it. He will have found a way to sneak out, his noises masked by the highway drone. An old, dormant wisteria vine climbs outside Thea's window; she hopes he has enough sense to leave through the front door.

Pilar falls back asleep and dreams about her daughter vomiting into the toilet, as she once did. The predictability of this dream makes her bolt upright in a full sweat. Pilar listens to the sounds of the highway: the thick madness of seven-thirty; she's late. She listens for noise in Thea's room, remembering Robbie. She hopes he got out safely. She hopes he doesn't get caught in lies.

Lissa Franz lives in Concord, Massachusetts, with her husband and three young children. She is currently completing a collection of short stories. This is her second published story.

SEEDS/*Catherine MacCarthy*

(for Roger and Siobhan)

My father's hands
scatter grain, freckled,
giant, as I stumble after him
watching his palms
cast from a jute sack
this way and that as if
he's performing a rite.
And what I wonder about is
how he measures out
the ground and how he knows
how thick and fast to plant
as he paces forward
and where exactly it lands?
The Bible warns against stones.
What about the birds
already having a feast
as they flock and lift
treating our harrowed space
as if it were Christmas?

He's unconcerned about stones
and it's important to cater
for the birds. They'll soon
have enough. As for the seeds
I watch them sprout
delicate ribby greens
against the rainy earth
and rise over months to a deep
aquamarine that glistens
and runnels under the breeze.
Avid to catch the split
second the colours change
I play hide and seek
vanish and appear,

eye to eye with ripening grain
stilled by a tide shifting
the field and close my eyes
to listen as the harvest
turns golden.

DELUGE/*Catherine MacCarthy*

In the house next door are two small boys.
They throw Beanie Babies across the fence

and shout their names and call for someone
to throw them back. I sit quiet with a book

pretending not to exist as animals rain
but they have climbed onto a ledge and spied

a patch of dress through the lattice and red
roses that bloom all round a gap in the hedge.

Already there are lions, elephants, penguins,
and several species of reptile looking sad.

"Here's Amber," they holler undeterred.
A striped cat lands at my feet.

Two pairs of brown eyes observe.
"Would you like to keep him?" They smile

as I pick up the cat. Amber is soft, enough
to take me off guard. More Beanies shower

the fence. The boys are yelling and it's time
for bed but from their incessant voices,

I can hear that exhaustion is a deluge
flooding the land, their parents are already

drowned and I am beginning to understand
what Noah in the ark must have felt:

I am their only chance and my garden
is the last high island left.

THE FREEDOM OF THE CITY / *Catherine MacCarthy*

He slips out the back gate
with a young woman,
fair hair, pouting lips
and long ethnic skirts,

an old man with keys in his hand,
his bald head turned
to check the lie of the land,
that one backward glance

cautious as the bushy-tailed
red fox whose eyes met mine
in our garden after rain
one November afternoon

in a deluge of green
between leaf fall and sunshine
before he turned to light again
high on the boundary wall.

ISLAND OF MIRACLES/*Catherine MacCarthy*

Forty degrees. Not a soul on the beach.
I began to dream of rain
as we lay in our shuttered room,
blood growing thin,

of standing out in a field
drenched to the skin, tongue out
drinking as it poured down,
of falling to my knees before the heavens.

We sped north and east,
the hot wind from Africa burning our heels,
rose with the road, with our fear,
the breath of an angry god

through mountains above a ravine
round Kera Pass,
you could no longer steer
and our bike was a trembling reed.

I turned my face from the precipice
as you steadied the wheel
in that land of the mother goddess,
and drove at full throttle.

I could feel our lives in our hands,
then mercy of the elements
as we flew to the plain
of a thousand springs

where the gale ceased
by the cave of baby Zeus,
and we glimpsed the shadow
of an eagle floating downstream.

Catherine MacCarthy's first collection, *This Hour of the Tide,* was published in 1994, and her second, *The Blue Globe,* in 1998. "Word of Mouth," a third collection, is near completion. She was awarded Arts Council bursaries for poetry in 1994 and 1998. Her poems have been published in anthologies and reviews in Ireland and the U.S.

EMERITUS/*Jill Marquis*

BEHIND BUILDING 400, I watched an elderly man in a very worn, untucked button-down shirt and a pair of thin, light blue shorts shuffle around the back of a delivery truck. He wore loafers with white socks. His head jutted forward as he peered at the truck parked in the loading dock. He circled the truck slowly, looking up at it the whole time. It was a white seventeen-footer, and the words *Metal Fabrication Incorporated* were painted in plain black lettering on its sides. Almost an entire minute elapsed as the old man made his way around the truck, and then, although it did not seem possible, he slowed down even more. He reached out, and it looked like he might tip over. But then his hand came to rest on the trunk of a large blue family sedan. He sighed. His car was blocked in. He looked around helplessly. He met my eyes without, I could tell, really seeing me. I had met him once before and managed to remember his name: "Dr. Sarafian," I said, "what's up? Is that your car?"

"What the hell is going on around here?" he said. "I don't know what the hell is going on."

I didn't know what to do, so I went back inside the building to get someone. The first person I saw was Dr. Paul. He was hunched over his desk, applying a screwdriver to the back panel of a clock radio. He looked determined and happy—it was a scene straight out of *Popular Mechanics*. I had a sort of eldercrush on Dr. Paul. At the time I was twenty-five but did not feel well. It seemed to me that I hadn't felt quite right for years, that I was not properly enjoying my youth. I needed to be distracted from myself, so I thought a lot, maybe too much, about the tiny old men who tottered through my world. *Emeritus* was an enchanting word—it sounded like a perfume, and being one seemed to require very little effort, just occasional walking to and from cars and sitting in chairs. Nothing was expected of the emeriti. I wanted to rest on my laurels instead of sitting on my ass, but I had none.

Building 400 was the most decrepit building in University Research Park. Everyone there was either old or horribly disabled in some way. (Like, there was one guy who was young and appeared to be normal but always looked to the left or right whenever I talked to him. It seemed that he had a blind spot just my size.) Of all the old men, Dr. Paul was the cream of the crop. Dr. Paul was practically elderhot. He always seemed to be dressed for a Boy Scout jamboree, minus the scarf and regalia. It was all about the khaki shorts and the can-do attitude.

He wasn't particularly physically attractive—that is not part of elder-hotness. "Dr. Paul," I said, "Dr. Sarafian needs your assistance outside."

He craned his neck and looked at me. He had a way of looking at a girl that did not involve heavy-handed assessment but was nevertheless quite appreciative. His eyes brightened. The way he talked was very Disney, sort of corny but charming. "Carol! How are you? What seems to be the problem?"

"Dr. Sarafian's car is blocked in."

"Okay, madame, I am ready to help. Lead the way."

We walked out together and paused on the loading dock. We watched Dr. Sarafian climb into the cab of the truck. During the ascent, one of his loafers fell to the ground. He situated himself with some difficulty, then got the door to close. He sat there for a minute and grumbled, "Where the hell is it?"

I slipped around to the passenger side, climbed in and asked Dr. Sarafian what he was looking for. He did not reply. Dr. Paul approached the driver's-side window and negotiated with Dr. Sarafian for a minute, then handed Dr. Sarafian his loafer. "Here you go, sir! Sit tight. I'll get your car out," he said.

Then he headed off, jingling Dr. Sarafian's car keys. It didn't look like he was going to be able to free the car. Dr. Sarafian stroked the vinyl seat and looked out the window. He tucked his downturned hands under his mostly bare thighs. Through the thin shorts I could see the faint outline of his you-know-what. It is embarrassing to mention this because I didn't mean to look, but there it was—not much to see but unsettling all the same.

We sat there. A group of subjects exited the building: young men of average builds wearing identical sneakers. They stood on the loading dock smoking, trying to center themselves before the next round of testing began. They were subjects in Dr. Paul's artificial-horizon study. The theory was that people on ships wouldn't feel seasick if they could just see a horizon at all times. The results were not yet final, but those boys didn't look well.

Dr. Sarafian turned his attention to the instrument panel. He dusted it off. He ran his hand along one side of the steering column, then down the other. The keys were right there, dangling from the ignition. I thought about taking them but did not. Out my window, I watched Dr. Paul back up Dr. Sarafian's car a few inches, crank the wheel, inch forward a few inches, then back up again. He did it again, and again, and as a result was wedged in as tightly as he had been before, only at a worse angle.

Then Dr. Sarafian found the keys in the ignition. He grabbed hold of them. "Hey," I said, "I don't think you should do that. *Hey.*"

He started the truck. It lurched forward a few feet, and I thought he might stop, but he didn't. He turned onto the main drive of the office campus, then proceeded to Speedway Boulevard, a major thoroughfare. Without pausing or checking for traffic, he turned right onto the boulevard. Loose pieces of fabricated metal clattered around in the back of the truck. I fastened my seatbelt and watched the passenger's-side mirror, hoping that Dr. Paul would give chase.

For a second I thought I saw Dr. Paul in the mirror, but then suddenly there were a lot of cars all around us, and all of them were going faster than us. Dr. Sarafian was unruffled by the traffic and unworried about his role in it. He went east a little ways, then north, then south, then west, meandering through neighborhoods, sticking to the surface streets. He maintained a steady pace of about fifteen miles per hour, so there was plenty of time to see everything. Cars kept passing us.

Riding in a big truck feels sort of like floating—the suspension is slow-bouncing and the steering loosey-goosey. However, as the truck was not actually floating, all I could think was: Thank God nobody walks anywhere anymore. Thank God there are no pedestrians loitering in crosswalks. But soon I noticed that people actually do walk anymore. They walk along narrow streets that don't have sidewalks; they walk by schools and day cares and grocery stores. They stand a few feet from the curb, out in the middle of the street, watching for the bus. It is a freaking code-red situation out there.

There are six degrees of freedom: surge, sway, yaw, pitch, heave and roll, and inside Building 400 there was a marvelous contraption that could simulate all of them. Eight times a day a subject ascended the platform and spent a half hour standing there holding a baton horizontally while the device pitched and yawed beneath him. The subject's task was to stand still, avoid "tripping events" and try not to ralph. The technicians changed the mix of yaw and roll every few days in an effort to determine what type of motion was most provocative. In the next building, Dr. Sarafian had spent much of his career tackling the problem of rust.

While he drove, Dr. Sarafian did not tell me interesting things about his life or share folksy wisdom of any sort. He did not seem to remember I was there, even though I kept saying, "Hey" and "Um," and making weak suggestions about stopping. I said things like, "How about some ice cream?" and "Radio Shack!" and coughed quite frequently.

Dr. Paul had once told me that if you ever feel like you are having a heart attack it is a good idea to cough because that sort of kicks your heart into motion again. He had been a heart surgeon and a fighter pilot and was devoting his golden years to the problems of provocative motion. Provocative motion is the motion of the ocean, and the main problem with it is that it makes even the strongest men queasy. My job was to schedule the subjects, do the interviews and write the reports. As a result, the only young men I talked to on an average day were either nauseous or about an hour away from being nauseous.

We passed my old middle school, which was letting out for the day. I reached for the wheel, certain that Dr. Sarafian was going to mow someone down, but then he stopped at the light, so it was okay. Children who were surprisingly small streamed out of the school as we waited at the light there. At least *I* was waiting for the light. Dr. Sarafian appeared to be just sitting there. The light turned, and still he sat there. I thought about nudging him, but it seemed wrong, like I would be interrupting him. Finally, I reached over and tapped the horn. He resumed driving.

He was slow to stop, quick with the horn. On major streets, he changed lanes slowly, frequently, for reasons I could not discern. He was intent on driving, and after a while I felt slightly better because although I had no idea where we were going, he appeared to know what he was doing except at stoplights. Shortly Dr. Sarafian crossed the freeway, and we entered my old neighborhood. I saw my old piano teacher's house. We passed a woman pushing a stroller who looked a lot like my best friend from second grade. My life flashed before my eyes at fifteen miles per hour: we passed my high school; we passed my favorite record store; we passed the spot where I once stood up Matthew Goerkel, a boy who was unbearably sweet. We passed my apartment building, the site of several of my ongoing experiments in solo living. At the time, I was pursuing three main lines of inquiry: (a) What would happen if you didn't open your mail for a few months? (b) What would happen if you put all the dirty dishes in the fridge? Would that stall the growth of mold indefinitely? and (c) If you really liked grapefruit and ate enormous amounts of it daily, would that be a problem?

We passed the video store, where I rented movies alone almost every night, and the grocery where I bought large quantities of vitamins and beer. We passed the nice-looking neighborhood bar, the one with all the windows that I often strolled past but never entered. Then I thought I saw an old boyfriend who had left town a year ago. What was he doing outside the mall, dressed like a bum? I flipped my hair back, sort of fixed it, then realized it wasn't him at all.

After a while, Dr. Sarafian got sidetracked onto a narrow road near the expressway that gradually became less and less of a road. The pavement stopped; then the gravel stopped; then we were bouncing along over a series of alarmingly large craters. The clankety-clank of fabricated metals filled the cab of the truck. Forlorn couches, busted-out televisions and trash crowded the sides of the lane. We heaved along until the lane was just a path, and then the truck almost stopped. Dr. Sarafian paused thoughtfully for the first time since he'd gotten into the truck. He considered the terrain. I sensed that he was on the verge of noticing me. A stand of tall weeds mixed with slim saplings blocked our way. "What the hell is that?" he said. Then he rolled over it. We were on a real road again! "Okay," he said.

We had arrived in a part of town I hadn't been to before, full of strip malls and cul de sacs that seemed familiar but were not. A water tower hovered over the neighborhood, standard issue but painted bright orange. It said Grove Heights, even though there were no heights anywhere around. Dr. Sarafian passed the water tower, then took a left off the main drag and went down a tree-lined street. After a few blocks, he pulled over in front of a modest split-level house and turned off the ignition. I jumped out immediately and hurried around the truck to help him out. When I opened the door, the loafer fell out, so I picked it up and put it on his foot. I felt like a valet. I looked at the loafer in a satisfied and efficient way. "That's more like it."

I held my arms out, offering to help him down, but he waved me away. Then he changed his mind; he really leaned on me getting out, and we both almost fell down. It was weird; he kept holding on to my hand. We stood there a second, then started walking toward the house together, hand in hand. It seemed the polite thing to introduce myself. "What's your name?" I asked quietly.

"Sarafian," he said.

"It's nice to meet you. My name's Carol. Is this your house?"

"Yes."

"Do you think I could use your restroom?"

Dr. Sarafian guessed so. He was docile, and faintly romantic, but had a surprisingly strong grip. At the door I realized he didn't have his keys. I rang the bell, and a minute later a woman answered. Although she was wearing a sort of nurselike housecoat uniform, it was plain that she was his wife. Her eyes flickered over me, the truck, the absence of the family sedan, then rapidly came into focus on Dr. Sarafian, her personal emeritus. "Oh!" she said, exhaling. "Come in! You're okay, aren't you?" She extricated him from my arm, and he leaned on her.

"He's tired," she said to me. "Thank you for getting him here. They took his license."

"It was nothing," I said.

She murmured reassuring things and led him to the bedroom so he could get some rest. I stood awkwardly in the foyer. Their immaculate house, full of pictures and belongings, could not have been more different from my own. I waited several minutes for Mrs. Sarafian's return.

Then I went to the restroom. Afterward, I used their phone to call work and reached Dr. Paul, who was eager to come get me. I started to tell Dr. Paul about Dr. Sarafian's visionquest, but that felt rude, so I stopped, said I'd tell him later. I was still alone, so I took a look around. In the Sarafians' garage I found one of those mini-trampolines people used to use for exercise. I stepped onto it and began to bounce. I surged, I pitched, I even yawed. For a while I thought about nothing in particular, but then I started to form a few feelings. They were strangely optimistic, about the future—about a world crowded with people en route to definite destinations, a world in which even I would stride along swinging my arms, brimming with purpose. I continued to bob for a while, then walked outside to the curb and sat there until Dr. Paul arrived in the emancipated family sedan. I did not exactly feel well but no longer felt ready to retire.

Jill Marquis earned an MFA in writing from the University of Montana. Her work has appeared in the *Mississippi Review, McSweeney's* and other journals. She lives and works in New Orleans.

SOCIAL DISCOURSE, 1944/*Jane Eaton Hamilton*

H ELLO," SAID BOBBY Houston. He was slight, with wire-rimmed glasses over pale, almost white-blue eyes. He had a nervous tic—his left hand jabbed out. She could see through his skin.

"You're the replacement milkman," said Alice.

"Here to serve you, ma'am," said Bobby and doffed his cap. Wispy hair surrounded him like a halo.

"Milton's in Paris right now," Alice said. "I believe."

"Four-F on account of my stutter," Bobby said. The word "stutter" refused to come out until he'd taken about four whacks at it, during which time his cheeks, formerly white as aspirin tablets, turned the colour of beets.

Alice said, "Isn't it funny that I'm on my own husband's route?" She looked out through the sleet at the roadway. Taffy, her husband's dapple-grey mare, put her head up and stepped forward so the cart carrying the milk bottles clanked. "Taffy'll be wanting her apple."

"One quart of Golden Guernsey!" said Bobby Houston, unloading it onto the speckled Arborite of Alice's kitchen table. He had trouble with the 'g's.' "Guaranteed tuberculin free. Twelve percent more solids. Superior flavour. One-third more cream." He lifted a bar of butter. "One pound saltless creamery butter. One pint virgin whipping cream." V-v-v-v-virgin. The tip of his nose was red with cold; his natty blue jacket dripped with rain. "Liquid health," he said and saluted. "You can't wash milk! If you knew the hazards that beset milk cleanliness you would insist on knowing your dairy. Take no chance with the milk you drink. Phone Michael 8944 and order Mountain Dale better milk delivered to your home." M-m-milk. Ho-ho-home.

Alice laughed and plucked Tracey from the playpen. Bobby Houston made faces at the baby, and she giggled wildly.

Bobby Houston took to stopping after every delivery; it felt as good to Alice as if her brother were visiting. Alice had not been prepared for married life—for the sex, Milton's absence, the pregnancies, the child—and Bobby reminded her of an easier time, when she flirted with boys as a matter of growing up, when she flashed her teeth and shook her hair, when she worried her stockings up her legs wrinkle by wrinkle. Now there weren't stockings and she used eyebrow pencil to draw lines up the backs of her legs like everyone else, only they always wavered. She'd taken to leaving them off. Why not? Who was to see?

Her mother and her sister were in Saskatchewan. Her father was dead. Her husband was at war. Bobby Houston was deeply familiar—he had Milton's smell (horse sweat, hoof trimmings and sour milk), Milton's sharp uniform, the same bottle caddy, the same spit-polished shoes. The same route boss, the owner's son Maurice Maclean. Maurice called every week to see how she was getting along. Just a courtesy, the way the dairy had other courtesies: a sewing group for the troops; picnics and parties.

Alice knew she shouldn't have Bobby Houston over every afternoon, that people would talk. But he seemed to like her, and the baby loved him, and when Alice's ankles were throbbing he lifted them into his lap and massaged them until the bloating rose back up her legs. There were no improprieties. Alice didn't feel about Bobby the way she felt about Milton, and Bobby didn't feel that way about her either, she was certain.

He told her things about the Maclean brothers, who ran the dairy, how Dave Maclean had chewed out Diane at the switchboard, making her cry (no news there—Milt had told similar stories of Dave Maclean's bullying); how he'd seen Patrick Maclean's wife taking stationery from the supply cupboard and dropping it into her purse—pads and pencils and erasers; how he had bumped into Maurice Maclean, his immediate boss, at the corner getting a shave. He swabbed at his head when he told Alice this last—his stutter was worse than ever, and the tips of his ears flared red as crayons. He wanted to know what Alice knew about Maurice Maclean, but Alice didn't know much. He was the bachelor brother in the family; he lived with his aging mother; he seemed to have a special fondness for horses. He always remembered the name of Alice's baby, along with the date of Alice's wedding anniversary. Milton thought highly of him. Alice shrugged. Talking about the Maclean brothers was like talking about the constellations in the sky—they were there, above everybody, but not touchable. They didn't keep her warm when she was lonely for Milton.

Poor, pale Bobby. His eyes lit up as if he had fever. "Because I think he likes me."

"Of course he likes you, Bobby. Doesn't everyone like you?" This was far from true, as Alice was learning. Bobby was becoming a topic of conversation. Her mother-in-law, the dairy wives, everyone had something mildly unpleasant to say about him. Little things Alice was certain were contrived—that he'd left Nellie's blinders and bridle on overnight; that he'd come up a dollar short in his reckonings; that he'd been observed lurking outside the ladies' washroom.

"Let me clean up these dishes for you," said Bobby and jumped to his feet, his glasses sliding down his nose.

Alice couldn't help but let him. Bobby in his crisp, blue, ironed milkman's uniform sang show tunes as he scrubbed, and he didn't stutter at all. As for Alice, she hadn't had much sleep. She'd been up half the night with Tracey, and now the baby inside was restless, kicking her inside out. Bobby was Alice's consolation. She found herself laughing uproariously while they played gin rummy, say, or when he told risqué jokes. Everything got easier.

Soon Bobby was coming for supper every night, carrying groceries in paper sacks up the driveway after he got off work. He cooked dishes like duck à l'orange and vichyssoise. He said it was a miracle they'd found each other. He said he'd never had a good friend before, that he was always the boy everyone made fun of. "Because of my stutter," he said mournfully. Alice said people had always laughed at how ungainly *she* was in gym class.

"Oh, me too!" cried Bobby. He lifted a wine glass full of milk in a toast. "You really are my friend."

Alice clinked her glass. "I haven't had a real friend since I was in high school."

"I get so lonely. Do you get lonely, Alice?"

Alice didn't know what to admit and what not to admit. She supposed she was happy with Milton; she *was* happy with Milton, just—She was happy with Tracey, too . . . mostly. Finally, Alice nodded. It seemed a brave admission. "I've been less lonely lately, though."

"Oh," said Bobby. "I'm so glad!" And he rose and massaged her shoulders.

Bobby confided to Alice that he liked to vacuum and dust and especially spread floor wax—then asked if she minded because his apartment was as small as a shoebox, with nothing to shine. Really, she'd be doing him a favour. It wasn't hard to say okay. Alice stretched out on the couch with the small, crammed space that was her stomach full of rich French food and a cold compress on her forehead, with Tracey down for the night, and watched him as he ran a feather duster over the table she and Milton had bought in Richmond. He kept up a patter about Maurice Maclean while he worked—how he'd bumped into Maurice at the bowling alley, how he'd seen him at the grocery store with his old mother, how he'd run into him taking his shirts to the cleaners.

Alice lifted onto her elbows; the compress slid into her hair and fell to the floor. "Why do you talk about Maurice Maclean so much?"

Bobby Houston's back stiffened, and the feather duster gave off an irritated vibration.

Alice sat up. Her stomach was getting huge. She was only seven and a half months, but she weighed exactly what she'd weighed with Tracey at birth. She'd been to the doctor, and he'd told her to go on a diet if she didn't want the baby to be an imbecile. Plus, the doctor said, she was flirting with a lifelong weight problem. That was probably why she had the headache. She could imagine a horrible future where Milton came home from the war a decorated hero, took one look at his immense wife and cut out on her. She looked at the man across the room who wasn't her husband, and for the first time in the weeks since he'd started coming around, she got a whiff of how odd it was to have Bobby Houston dusting her knickknack shelves.

"What are you saying?"

"I barely know Maurice Maclean, that's all, and I get a little tired of hearing about him. I'm so tired." Alice could hear Tracey starting to fuss. "I think I've been tired since the day I was born."

Bobby Houston turned, an odd smile across his lips. "I will never get tired of Maurice Maclean," he said. He stuttered over the '*m*'s'. Then he said, "Do you need your windows washed, Alice, by any chance? Because I picked up this new product by the Johnson and Johnson people and I've been longing to give it a go."

Of all the dairy wives, Alice liked one woman, the wife of another milkman, the best. Ginger was everything a Ginger should be—brassy, loud, industrious. But Ginger was already saddled with four kids under the age of six. "I'm going out of my mind!" she'd shout. "I'd like to get together, of course I would, but Alice, I'm snowed under. I honestly am. Maybe we can have tea. Next week, or the week after that, when things here are more under control—" And Alice would hang up the telephone receiver and feel the silence of her own home echoing. It was the only time she actually wanted the baby to cry, just to hear a human voice.

"I brought dress-up?" Bobby announced one night. D-d-d-ress-uh-uh-up. He pulled skirts and high heels and hats and slips from an Eaton's bag and tossed some over to her. "Put these on."

"These?" Alice lifted a man's suit coat, a tie, wool trousers. "No, I won't. I can't. I wouldn't dare."

"We'll have fun. Please? Pretty please?"

But Alice refused, only giving in enough to plonk a hat on Bobby, a red, ladies' chapeau with a mesh veil that could be brought down over the eyes.

There was a record on the radio in the living room—Jimmy Dorsey's orchestra—and Bobby pulled Alice to the floor to dance. She didn't know where he'd learned, but he knew everything—the Carolina Shag, Shim Sham, the Lindy Hop. His hat kept falling off. Even with her swollen ankles and her oversized belly, Alice tried to keep up. When the segment ended, they fell laughing onto the couch together and Alice, without thinking, said, "I just love you, Bobby Houston."

Bobby went quiet.

"I mean," said Alice. "I didn't mean—" She shook her head. She found herself telling secrets. She told him about her parents, how her father was the county vet and how her mother had longed to sing professionally and how there'd been three dead babies after Alice, and how her mother had wept the first decade of Alice's life and then refused to speak for seven more years. She hadn't started talking again until Alice was out of high school and standing at the door with her suitcase, ready to take a taxicab to the bus station and a future at a secretarial school in Birmingham, as far away as she could conceive of getting and where she had a cousin who would take her in. Alice said, "I knew I ought not to go. I knew she was talking again to keep me home, but I just had to get out of there." Alice also told Bobby about how she met a fresh boy on the bus and had to report him, about meeting Milton and falling in love and deciding to get married even though she'd vowed she'd be a spinster if marriage meant becoming as dry and used up as her mother. Shyly, she mentioned sexual intercourse, what a welcome surprise it had been to her and how she couldn't believe married couples *ever* got out of bed. She was a little embarrassed. To change the subject she said, "Now you. You tell me something scandalous."

But Bobby began to kiss her. He kissed her forehead with lips as soft and dry as insect wings. He kissed her eyebrows and her cheeks and her chin and the tip of her nose. Her heart beat hard. She didn't know how to take it. He threaded his fingers through hers, and when he looked up at her, his odd eyes were glassy with tears. "Alice, I wear—" he said and then stopped, his face flaming. He turned his head away from her and his voice dropped.

"Alice, sometimes I wear women's underwear."

Alice jerked her hand away, smoothed her skirt over her knees.

Bobby turned to look at her, eyes puffy with hope and fear. He said, "You hate me, don't you? I know you hate me." H-h-h-hate.

"How could I hate you?" Alice said, but the words were thick on her tongue. Of course he was right. The place where she loved him sprang a leak; all the affection drained right out. It wasn't hate that was left, however, but revulsion. He made her sick. She didn't even feel sorry for him, poor outcast, poor loser. She smoothed her skirt again as if he might try to look up it, and slowly stood. "It's late, Bobby," she said with a flat voice. "You should probably go home."

"I don't do it very often," Bobby said, springing up beside her like a puppy, his absurd ladies' hat tilting rakishly. "I hardly ever do it. Just once in a blue moon, when I clean—once a year, or once every two years, when I can't stop myself."

Alice lifted a hand to her sweating neck. "I don't know why you'd tell me such a thing, Bobby."

"I thought you'd under—"

"Understand?" she said. It was like saying you'd understand if a tornado hit southern Ontario. Of course she didn't understand. Bobby Houston was a pervert. She suddenly saw what other people saw when they looked at Bobby—an oddball, somebody who could never fit in and was pathetic for trying. "I think I hear Tracey. Can you let yourself out?"

Women's underwear! It made her shiver to think of it. She imagined his hairy legs, his belly, and then a pair of her underwear riding his hips—too tight, of course, because she was smaller and she didn't have all that—equipment—to fit. She looked in on Tracey, who was sleeping soundly, her fat cheeks moist, then went into her bedroom and counted the pairs of underwear in her drawer. Most of them were sensible white cotton panties that went up to her waist, but there were two pairs tucked at the back that Milton had brought home on leave from France. Lacy, tiny as hankies.

Alice got into her pajamas and sat in the den with her knees up listening to a radio play. She heard the front door, her mother-in-law calling, "Yoo-hoo! Alice, dear!" and bringing in a sack of groceries. Dress-up clothes were all over the floor, but Alice was immobilized.

"I got pot roast on special, Alice!" Then she noticed the scattered clothing. She bent to pick up a red lace slip. "Where did these things come from?"

"Um," Alice said, embarrassed and instantly ashamed.

"It's that milkman fellow, isn't it, that curious little thing from the Dairy?"

"Tracey and I were just . . ." But Alice petered out. Were just what? Playing dress-up?

"Dear, you can tell me."

So Alice did.

"Ginger?" said Alice on the telephone a few nights later when she thought loneliness would end up killing her. "Can I run something by you?"

"I have to get the children tucked in. It's an hour past their bedtimes. Can I call you back?"

"Would you? Would you call me back?"

"Of course I will," she said, but she did not.

Over the next days, Alice couldn't get rid of the picture of Bobby Houston in women's underwear. She imagined him in a bra, a girdle, a merry widow. She imagined him wearing lipstick, rouge and mascara; she imagined him teetering down the street swinging an alligator handbag. She made sure she and Tracey were out of the house—at the library, the market—when it was time for Bobby to deliver her milk. When she got home she'd discover bottles wedged between the screen door and the back door; once a week a bill was tucked in a pristine envelope.

Gradually, though, the picture of Bobby in women's underwear started wavering like a mirage on asphalt; the shock wore off. She remembered how much fun they'd had. She was ashamed she'd told Milton's mother, which was sure to stir the gossip pot. Without him, Alice's existence was as empty as her morning grapefruit rind. She didn't know how to fill her days. She couldn't store up outrageous things her mother-in-law said to tell him later; she couldn't show him how Tracey had learned to crawl with one leg stuck out straight behind her; she couldn't brag about the scarves she was knitting for the fighting men. She missed him. Bobby had only been confiding a weakness to her, as she had confided various weaknesses to him: that she sometimes dreamed of alternate kinds of husbands, for instance, with more exciting jobs than Milton's, who made more money than Milton did, who lived in more exotic places, like Toronto. Or that Milton hadn't been the first boy to kiss her. Bobby had believed he could trust her. Bobby had exposed himself to her, and she had reached right in and ripped out his heart, ripped away the only significant friendship he'd ever made—or for that matter, she'd ever made. So what if the man wore ladies' panties? As long as they weren't Alice's, why should she care? It didn't mean anything, except that people were complicated. Within a week, she had vowed to renew their friendship and this time never to let Bobby down. When she heard the clop of horse hooves on the street, she wrenched open the front door, grinning. But it wasn't Bobby delivering; it was Sam Bartholomew, a friend of Milton's, who said Bobby had been let go.

"Let go?" she said.

Sam said, "I've got his route for the next few weeks at least." He passed her over a quart of Golden Guernsey. "Hear from Milt?"

The milk was cold in her hand. She allowed as to how she'd gotten a letter with bits cut out by censors. "He's still in France, is all I know."

Sam eyed her belly. "You doing okay?"

Alice nodded. She didn't get any sleep because she couldn't get comfortable. She was getting purple bulges across her calves. Plus she had a network of stretch marks shimmering on her hips. She was huge, one sixty-six. She wanted Milton to come home. She wished Bobby, so handy and happy with chores, could go into labour for her.

She called the dairy for Bobby's address—Broadway East and Cordova. She wheeled Tracey over. There was litter in the gutters, debris blowing in the breeze down the sidewalks. All the buildings were red brick and square. Sixty-two, sixty-eight, seventy-four—those were all houses. Twelve fifty-six Broadway East was a six-plex, and Alice found Bobby—Robert Houston—listed beside the bell. Bobby stuck his head out a front window.

"It's me!" Alice called up, waving her handkerchief. "Me and Tracey."

"Go home!"

"I won't go home!"

"You can't come up!"

"Let me in, Bobby. I came all this way. My feet hurt."

"You hurt my feelings."

F-f-f-feelings. Alice looked around to make sure no one was in hearing distance. "Do you want the stork to come here in the street?"

He floated down a key on a long turquoise ribbon. She left the baby carriage on the street, hoping no one would pinch it. She climbed up three floors wearily, both babies heavy as potatoes. It was three in the afternoon, but Bobby was wearing a plaid robe and slippers.

She stood just outside his doorway, panting with exertion.

"You were really mean, Alice," said Bobby, with his chin absurdly high, his face half averted. His arms were clasped over his chest. "I would never be that mean to you."

"Give me a lemonade."

"No."

She shoved Tracey at him. He took her and let Alice pass. The apartment surprised her. She'd expected it to be dingy and dim, but it wasn't. It was tiny but bright and orderly. Pin neat. The furniture wasn't expensive, but it was nicely set out, with two easy chairs across from a deep chesterfield. There was a working fireplace, with logs snapping and crackling. The walls were kelly green.

Alice pulled a pair of panties she'd stopped for at Eaton's from her diaper bag and dangled them, grinning.

At once Bobby thawed, as if he hadn't really been mad. He took on a girlish openness. "Oh, Alice!" he cried and snatched the underwear. "You're wonderful. I missed you like strawberries in January! Did you miss me?"

"I did."

"Did you?"

"I did! I really did! I'm sorry we fought."

"I'm tickled pink that you're here," said Bobby. "You won't believe what happened." He bustled around straightening newspapers at the table, moving a coffee cup aside, asking her if she'd like some tea. "Water's hot." When he bent to put a stack of magazines on the coffee table, his robe parted and Alice caught a flash of hot pink. She bit her bottom lip. "I heard."

"Oh, god, *what*?"

"Your job."

Bobby frowned. "Oh, my *job*! No, not that. Something wonderful. Something better than wonderful. It's about Maurice." He brought in teacups rattling on saucers, a bowl of sugar cubes with silver tongs, a small pitcher of cream.

"What? What?"

"Maurice *sacked* me."

"Well, yes, I heard."

"I had to sign a letter of resignation."

Alice widened her eyes and tilted her head forward.

"He pulled me into his office with some twaddle—" T-t-t-twaddle. "—about embezzlement and how Dave wanted to sack me himself, only Maurice stepped in and said no, it was his duty as my immediate supervisor and how he hadn't wanted to fire me—he was right against it—but how since I was going anyway, at least he got to tell me, and to tell me how important I am to him and how he wants to keep seeing me!"

"To keep seeing you," said Alice.

Bobby poured, holding an index finger atop the teapot. "I am on top of the world!"

"But embezzlement!"

"My float was always short," said Bobby, waving this irritation away.

"Floats *are* always short," said Alice.

"There's a dance next week."

Alice nodded.

"You going?"

Alice wiggled her toes. They felt like small anchors on the ends of her feet. "I hadn't thought about it. I generally do, but—"

"Morale booster," said Bobby, then sighed and bit a nail. He peered at the damage. "Victoria Day. I was going to get my white trousers out of storage, but now . . ." He sighed elaborately. "I suppose I won't be invited. Can I trust you, Alice?"

Alice shrugged.

"I mean, really trust you?" Bobby laid a hand over his heart.

Alice nodded slowly.

"Cross your heart and hope to die."

She did it.

"The thing is," said Bobby slyly, "I had the weensiest bit of social discourse with Maurice outside the office."

Alice raised her brows. Tracey had gotten a sugar cube in her tiny fist and was sucking it through her fingers; Alice didn't bother to stop her.

"He took me to—we went to his club together. Had cocktails at the bar, dinner in the dining room. Did you know the Golf and Country Club has hotel rooms upstairs? For members' use only?"

"Hotel rooms?" said Alice. She was having trouble keeping up.

"And the next day he called me into his office and dismissed me."

Then it dawned on Alice what Bobby was telling her. "But men *can't.*" She stared at her lap.

"Can," said Bobby, winking as she looked up.

"And anyway, Maurice Maclean isn't—he's a bachelor. He lives with his mother."

"*Is.* Oh, deliciously is."

"You and Maurice Maclean? Together, the two of you *do*—" She could not say the word "it" or, heavens, bear to think about what "it" might entail.

"Oh, Alice, pumpkin, are you living in the Dark Ages?" Bobby snapped his fingers in her face and pushed his glasses up his nose. "This is good news. This is great news!"

This was worse than wearing ladies' panties, this perversion between her best friend and his boss, her husband's boss. She peered at Bobby. If he was her best friend, wouldn't he behave with common decency? He was the one she got to lean on when times were tough, and he got to lean on her, too, didn't he? Only what if—couldn't he have social diseases? Couldn't the baby maybe catch something? She scooped Tracey and held her close, while Tracey, naturally, reached out for Bobby. "Well," she said. "I see."

"I may be in love. Yes, Alice, finally in love!" Bobby rose and spun through the room, his housecoat flipping up when he twirled, showing off the ridiculous hot-pink lingerie.

"I don't see, actually," said Alice. There was a pause, during which Bobby beamed. "Love?" Alice muttered. "But he sacked you? You're out of a job?"

"But, if you can believe it, he's already phoned me. Twice. He wants another go-round. Maybe *he'll* fall in love with *me*! Bobby's willful hand flew out.

"Maurice Maclean," said Alice, and the name had an actual acrid taste on her tongue. What objection could she reasonably raise? "But Bobby, he's old enough to be your father."

"Yes," said Bobby with a blissful sigh.

"I don't think Milt would be pleased," Ginger said when Alice, over cookies and juice, mentioned that Bobby was coming around again. Ginger's kids and Tracey were screaming. Ginger had to yell to be heard, and she was only half paying attention. She kept pulling one or another child off the others, threatening time out, no dessert, sitting in the corner, early to bed. "Everybody's talking about him and you, too. Do you know what you're doing, Alice?"

"He's okay," Alice said. She was crossing her fingers in her lap because she worried she was telling a fib. "Really. He is. He's a good guy. I'm a good judge of character."

On Victoria Day weekend, the spring cold snap finally broke, and half the civilized world tilled and seeded victory gardens. Alice was bloated; she couldn't, didn't want to, do anything. She craved Milton. The baby was coming down with something—wasn't the baby coming down with something? She was slick with sweat and endlessly fussy. At the very least she was cutting teeth. Her bottom gum was inflamed, and when Alice ran her finger across it she could feel the sharp promontories of two teeth hiding there, about to pierce poor Tracey with the first great pain of her life. Alice had two teething rings and kept one in the icebox while Tracey sucked the other—quite avariciously, at times shaking her head and growling at it as if she were a puppy with a sock in its mouth. Alice knew she should be more sympathetic (she did sometimes glance at Tracey and melt with love and pity) but mostly she felt aggrieved. She didn't understand why Milton wasn't home at a time like this. She didn't understand why, when she was nearly nine months pregnant, she also had to have a cranky baby. Secretly, she resented the war effort. She didn't understand why Bobby, who'd said he'd be there at one to help her plant peas and carrots, was late. He'd been acting hooey all week, on her about the dance, asking did she think anyone would mind if he attended with her?

Yes, yes, she was going to the dance. No, no, she wasn't going. What did it matter?

"*Because*," Bobby had said on Wednesday, "if I can go as your date, I'll get to see Maurice. Wouldn't that be divine?" D-d-d-divine. "My Maurice. My sweet Maurice. My very own lovable scoogey-woogey Maurice."

Alice had closed her eyes.

"He took me to Toronto to the opera," Bobby said. "He took me to the steam baths."

"What steam baths?"

"We went to his club again," said Bobby. Then his tone darkened. "But he says I can't go to the dance *with* him. It wouldn't look proper."

"Well," said Alice.

"You don't *agree*?"

"I don't disagree, exactly," Alice had said carefully.

The telephone had rung while Bobby was still there. It was Maurice Maclean to see how she was getting along. She wrapped herself in the cord and said she was well. "Fine, thank you."

Bobby had bobbed beside her on the balls of his feet, mouthing, "Who is it?"

She'd turned away from him. "No, thank you, Mr. Maclean," she said, "there's nothing we need. Thank you for asking." She listened. "Yes, hopefully Milt will be home in time. It's wonderful that the Dairy is a family to us while Milton is away."

"That was him, wasn't it?" Bobby had said when she was off.

"He checks in on all the wives."

"Phone him back," Bobby had said. "Tell him I want to go to the dance."

"I can't," Alice had said. "Bobby, I'm sorry, but please understand. He's Milton's boss."

"Pretty please? Pretty please with a cherry on top?"

"It's just a dance, Bobby. It's no big deal."

"You take me then."

"I can't. I'm sorry." People would laugh and stare. People would be terrible to her, and to Bobby too.

Bobby had pushed out his lips and refused to look at her.

That had been three days ago, and now Alice forced herself to go outside, stuffed Tracey into her baby carriage and started banging at the ruins of last year's garden. It had been cool, but it hadn't rained. The hoe kept hitting stones, and when she looked around, she saw that

Tracey was about to fall out of the carriage. She righted her and wiped off her teething ring.

Bobby came rolling up the alley like a burr. She saw him from a block away but pretended she didn't.

"He shouldn't have fired me!" he said and swiped his cap from his head. When he was mad, his skin became even more translucent.

"Hello to you, too."

Tracey cooed delight and reached out for Bobby, but he ignored her.

"He didn't have any right. I could sue."

"I thought you liked it," said Alice. "I thought you said Maurice fired you so he could give you special treatment."

"That was my damned livelihood! What am I going to support myself on now!"

"Don't," said Alice. "Language. Tracey."

"I *will* sue him," cried Bobby. "I saw him again on Tuesday, the bastard."

Alice dropped the hoe and put her hands over Tracey's ears.

"Nothing. Nothing since then. Nada. Zilch." Maurice hadn't called. Hadn't sent flowers. Hadn't sent a note. Wouldn't answer calls Bobby made to the Dairy *or* his home. So Bobby had gone by his place, had lurked by his place (l-l-l-lurked) until finally Maurice came out, and when Bobby ran up to him, Maurice tossed him aside like an old banana peel.

"He wouldn't even look at me! He always loved to look at me, especially in underwear."

Alice didn't know what to say.

"I followed him, and you know what? There's someone else. He picked up a man with the biggest nose this side of Lake Huron." Bobby shivered. "An *ugly* man. A man probably *forty* years old. And he took him into the club." Bobby paused, and his pale eyes glittered. "Do I deserve this, Alice? Do I deserve to be thrown away like an old . . . Menstrual pad?" M-m-m-menstrual.

Alice gasped.

Bobby took her by the shoulders. She could smell his breath; vinegar, she thought, as if he'd spooned some onto his tongue and let it dissolve. "Did you decide if you're going to the dance?"

"Don't," said Alice. "I don't know. Let me go." She pulled away. She liked him better when he was carefree, like a girlfriend.

"I want to know whether *he's* there," said Bobby. "And what he's *wearing*. And whether he *drinks*. And whether he *dances*. *You* dance with him, Alice. Ask him about me."

The sun was making Alice woozy. "Come inside," she said.

"I can't," said Bobby. "I need to know if you're going. Are you going?"

"Come have some lemonade."

But Bobby vanished, jittering down the alley like debris in a wind-storm.

Alice thought Bobby would be back that afternoon or evening—maybe they'd have one of his fancy meals and she could gain another five pounds—but he didn't show up or telephone, then or the next day or on Victoria Day itself. That afternoon, so that Alice could have a lie-down, her mother-in-law took Tracey, but when the baby was gone, Alice, though she'd pulled on a negligée, couldn't sleep. The time without a baby shrieking seemed too precious to waste with uncon-sciousness. Instead, Alice lingered in front of her makeup mirror, which cut her reflection off above her breasts—Alice could pretend she wasn't pregnant, was young and free. She applied makeup heavily. Cream, foundation, concealer, eyeshadow, eyeliner, mascara, rouge, lipstick, carefully blotting. She even curled her eyelashes. She batted her eyes at herself. Maybe she would go to the dance. Her mother-in-law would keep Tracey, and Alice could cut the rug with—why, with Tom or Pete or George, Milt's 4-F coworkers. Their wives wouldn't mind sharing them out for a dance apiece. A sudden wave of nausea made her clasp the vanity.

When Bobby called, that was all he wanted to know: "Are you going? We had a deal, right? You're going?"

"What deal?"

"Say you're going, Alice. You must go."

"I don't feel so well, Bobby."

"I thought I could count on you."

"I think I might be sick, Bobby. I can't go to the dance."

"Go anyhow. Go for me. Alice, I'm begging you. You don't realize how important this is."

"No," said Alice. "I'm sorry, but no." She clasped her belly.

He slammed down the phone. Alice felt bloated and horrible, and she wondered whether she might be getting mild labour pains. She began to weep; she didn't know why. She got up and caught sight of herself in the mirror—she looked like a tart, for G-d's sake. She wet a washcloth and rubbed hard. Really hard, so that she took off not just her makeup but layers of her skin. She called her mother-in-law, begged her to keep Tracey and stayed in bed.

Bobby Houston blasted through her back door at a few minutes after midnight like a snapped electrical wire. Alice was heating a glass of milk to settle her stomach. Bobby tried but failed to impart something, stuttering the syllables "foe" and "fie."

She told him to compose himself. She worried that her nipples were showing through her nightgown or that Bobby might want to wear the garment for himself.

Bobby's glasses had a broken stem; his eyes bugged out of his head. What did Alice see there? Terror? Glee? A vein shook on his forehead. Two fingers jabbed out at nothing. His face was red. He'd been running and was out of breath.

"Telephone," he finally managed, and, "Fire."

The Dairy's dance? At Elk Hall? Just seven blocks from where they stood?

"People are falling!" Fa-fa-falling.

"What people?" yelled Alice. "What *people*?"

Later Alice wouldn't remember the blocks she and Bobby covered together, her housecoat flowing out behind her like a cape. But there were images that never faded: the wail, first, of fire trucks and ambulances, one of which roared past Alice and Bobby as they ran; the terrible heat that latched onto Alice's throat; the sight of smoke obscuring the tops of the apartment buildings; and then Elk Hall itself, a two-story brick building engulfed in flames. But this wasn't the worst. The screams and the sight of bodies littered around the cement, then tripping over someone's shoes, finding her friend Ginger's purse with its hasp open, its contents spilled and sooty. Stumbling around people, calling out the names of friends, finding Tom McIntyre blackened with smoke, his hair burnt off, clutching his leg where the femur poked through the fabric of his trousers, the white shattered bone like a fence post. Finding Ginger, at last, in a yard two yards over, where she'd apparently stumbled as she burned; bending over her. Ginger's skin had peeled like birch bark.

Ten people died, including Ginger, and forty-eight more were seriously injured. Maurice Maclean, the only one of the Maclean brothers to attend, was on the critical list. He'd broken both wrists, some ribs and his back, and his burns were third degree, covering one-quarter of his body. The flash fire had broken out in the cloakroom, but how or why it had started remained a mystery. It had exploded up the stairs just as a Paul Jones tune started to play—the last dance of the night. The seventy people who had managed to escape were either pushed or jumped twenty-five feet from the two small second-floor windows. The newspapers reported the toll of dead and dying like a telegram from some new war. All week Bobby sat in Alice's kitchen with the

Birmingham Daily and the Toronto papers, assiduously cutting out articles.

"Listen to this, Alice," he'd start and then read to her while she rocked Tracey.

"'Virginia Marstock, thirty-one, wife of John Eric, 233 East Avenue, daughter of Mr and Mrs. Michael Williams of this city, was deceased on the scene. She leaves four children, John Jr., Virginia Claire, Michael Bartholomew III and Patricia Anne. She was born to this city and had been a lifelong resident. She was a member of St. John's Presbyterian Church and is survived by, besides her husband, children and parents, two brothers Tom and Michael Jr., and three sisters, Jane, Lois and Margaret (Mrs. Earl Frawke).'" Fr-fr-fr-Frawke.

"Stop, Bobby! Stop! Ginger was my friend."

"But there's more. Listen. 'Funeral services were held this afternoon for Mr. and Mrs. Alexander J. Petrie, Mr. John McKenzie, Mr. and Mrs. Roy Fontaine and Mrs. John Marstock, six of the fire victims.'"

Alice shot up. "I know there was a funeral! I was there! What's wrong with you! Why must you torture me with this?" She was still wearing her good black dress, her sensible pumps. She pulled Tracey's head hard against her chest.

"'Margaret Crawford,'" Bobby went on, Cr-cr-cr-Crawford. "'Wife of James W. Muir, 12 Graham Avenue South, was born in Scotland and was in her forty-third year. She had lived in Birmingham for twenty-one years and was highly esteemed by her many friends throughout this district. Surviving, besides her husband, are one son and three daughters. The remains are resting at the J. G. Pearl Funeral home until ten-thirty o'clock Monday morning and will then be conveyed to St. John's Anglican Church for service at three o'clock. Interment will be made in the Freemont Cemetery.'"

"Shut up!" said Alice. "Can't you please for five minutes just shut up?"

"Ahh," said Bobby, reading. "They've removed a pail—" P-p-p-pail. "—into which people emptied cigarette butts. What do you think that means?" He took off his glasses, swabbed his face and examined the tape holding them together.

"Can't you please?" said Alice grabbing the newspapers. Ten dead, five funerals, twelve orphans. Bobby went on and on—Elk Hall had been ordered to put in a fire escape, but building materials had been in short supply with the war. Guess who was still on the critical list? And who Bobby couldn't get in to see? "Even though we're so close," said Bobby. "They just discount that. They say, 'Family only,' as if family means so much."

Bobby stumbled in one afternoon saying he'd finally gotten in to see Maurice and it was true; he hung by a spidery thread to life ."He didn't know me!"

"He's in critical condition," said Alice flatly and went back to cutting onions.

Bobby went into a pout.

"I'm making stew," said Alice. She turned to look at him. "Did you notice? The peas have germinated. When I planted the seeds, Ginger was alive."

Bobby crossed his arms over his chest.

"My mother-in-law's coming for dinner, Bobby. You have to go."

Bobby unfolded himself. "Here's what they're about to announce: It was arson."

"What do you mean it was arson?"

"The fire. Someone set it."

"Don't be ridiculous."

"Joe Ferrare with the *Chronicle* told me. They're going to announce that it started in the burlap cover of a chair in the cloakroom. It took thirty seconds to engulf the stairwell, Alice. Thirty seconds! I wish I'd seen that!" Bobby's glasses glinted.

Alice turned to confront him. "Didn't you see enough, Bobby? Didn't you get a good enough look when people were falling from the windows like human torches?" She could feel her bottom lip curling. "Bobby, my best friend died. I knew every one of those ten people, Bobby, and all the rest that are still suffering. I was almost *at* that dance. Okay? Get out. Go home. Go get a job."

"But Alice," Bobby said and subsided into a chair.

"Out. I mean it," said Alice. She pointed at the door with her chopping knife.

Bobby said, "You don't mean get out."

"I do mean get out. Get out, Bobby Houston, get out and don't come back!" She stabbed at the air with the knife. "You're perverted and you're morbid and I hate how you keep rubbing this in. I just hate it. Go!"

"Alice, you don't mean it."

"I do mean it, Bobby! Go."

And Bobby went.

Alice couldn't get out of bed. The pregnancy wiped her out. Her eyes fluttered open to the sound of Tracey fussing in her crib, hungry and wet, and then fell shut. Finally she came to consciousness because her mother-in-law was shaking her shoulder.

"Alice, wake up. Get up. We need to talk."
Tracey was crying at the top of her lungs.
"All this time it was Bobby Houston."
"What? Bobby? What happened to Bobby?"
"He's in jail."
"Bobby?"

At that moment a labour pain hit; Alice didn't really care. Bobby set the fire? she thought. Bobby, a murderer? A conviction came over her as the contraction grew: if she had gone to the dance, no one would have died. Or would Bobby have tried to kill her, too?

Vaguely, she was aware of her mother-in-law gathering diapers and clothing, of her mother-in-law lifting Tracey from the crib. Alice pulled up her nightgown, and she and her mother-in-law watched as her stomach forced itself upwards into the shape of an egg. The pain began, but Alice noticed it only at a remove. She thought: Alice is in labour. Alice is about to have a second baby.

The baby was a boy, a seven-pound, fourteen-ounce soldier with wisps of black hair that stood out from his scalp. He didn't giggle as Tracey always had, but seemed rather to have been born carrying a burden. He grew up to be an accountant for the Royal Bank and married when he was only twenty-one years old—the same week, in fact, that Bobby Houston died in jail. Maurice Maclean, badly disfigured, didn't return to work at the Dairy, his interest bought out by his older brother. He made a killing playing the horses and on the stock market. He lived with his mother at first, then moved into a high rise on Franklin Street with a financier named Mr. Gilhooley.

Milt came home from the war when Michael was two months old. He heard all the details about Bobby Houston from his mother, but he acted as if he had not. He settled back into their old life and let Alice and the children settle back into it alongside him. Breakfast at six; a quick cup of tea together when he delivered their milk in the afternoon; dinner promptly at five. Pork chops, ham steaks and spaghetti once each week; fish on Fridays; pot roast on Sundays after church. When little Tracey saw Bobby Houston's mugshot in the newspaper, she snatched at it, crumpling it, but whether it was to bring Bobby Houston back or to send him further away, Alice never figured out.

Jane Eaton Hamilton is the author of six books, most recently a short-story collection *Hunger*, nominated for the Ferro-Grumley Award for best 2002 lesbian fiction. Her stories have appeared in the *Journey Prize* anthologies, *Best Canadian Short Stories* and elsewhere. She is working on a novel, "Wild Mare."

INTRODUCTION

"The Swan" was written when Thomas Lanier Williams, age twenty-eight, had just reinvented himself as "Tennessee." Under this name in 1939 he had finally had a story accepted by *Story* magazine, a Holy Grail for young writers, and had sent to a Group Theatre contest four plays that would earn him his first playwriting award. The contest was limited to writers under twenty-five, so he subtracted from his age the three "wasted" years from 1933 to 1935, when his father, a sales manager for International Shoes, had made him quit college to work as a clerk in the company factory. It was the Great Depression, and jobs were hard to find, but to Tom, the aspiring writer just beginning to achieve recognition, typing shoe orders eight hours a day was his "season in Hell." It took a nervous breakdown and recuperation with his grandparents in Memphis to free him once more to write. He had been reared by his grandparents during the seven years of his childhood when his father was a traveling salesman. Tom's grandfather, an Episcopal clergyman, was his role model, and his grandmother was the angel who through his penniless years would stitch five-dollar bills into her letters to him. In addition to falsifying his age to enter the Group contest, Tom had adopted his grandfather's house number in Memphis as his mailing address. Although he typed "Tennessee Williams, Memphis, September 1939" at the end of this story, he was not in Memphis that September but in New York City to meet his new-found agent and to study the professional theater firsthand.

Whether "The Swan" was written in the YMCA in New York or earlier, in the hot attic of his parents' home, it is a St. Louis story. Forest Park with its zoo, lagoon and pavilion is the setting for two strangers' adventure on a summer night. Williams builds up an atmosphere of stifling heat—a metaphor for his character's feeling of suffocation and his need to escape the domestic tyranny of lace curtains and the sleeping wife whose curled fingers make him think of "moist flowers of the insectivorous kind." Fleeing to the nearby park, he meets a girl equally desperate for relief. As they sit in darkness by the lagoon and the girl tells her story, their mutual understanding peaks in a violent moment that is cooled by the passing whiteness of a swan. Any possible story-book finish is dispelled by irony, although each character is allowed a small revelation.

"The Swan" is one of several stories the young Williams wrote that would feed into *The Glass Menagerie*, the work that made him famous overnight. The story anticipates the desperation of that play's Tom—the would-be writer confined to a boring job in "that celotex interior" and bound to a nagging mother and a sister who lives in a dream world of mental delusion. Laura in *The Glass Menagerie*, with her thwarted love, seems an extension of the girl in "The Swan." Both can be seen as portraits of Williams's own sister, Rose. The portrait of his mother, Amanda, in that play is a considerably softened version of the sickly, clinging wife in "The Swan." Both story and play address the themes of confinement and escape present in most of Williams's early work.

Williams would remain the rare writer who produced poetry, fiction and drama all his life. "The Swan" displays characteristics of all three genres in its poetic descriptions, suspenseful narrative and dramatic climax. It is typical of Williams's work habits that two years later he expanded his short story into a full-length play, *Stairs to the Roof*; in Scene 10 of that play, the girl's confessional monologue from "The Swan" is reproduced word for word. Striving for the sort of commercial success he had seen on Broadway, Williams disposed of the clinging wife, developed the couple's chance meeting into a boy-girl romance and conceived what may have been the only happy ending he would ever write. The play never made it to Broadway, but since the year 2000 it has been produced successfully several times. Perhaps the story's real significance is as a study for the playwright's first masterpiece, *The Glass Menagerie*.

—Allean Hale

THE SWAN / *Tennessee Williams*

IT HAD BEEN LIKE THIS for the past few nights, breathlessly still and overpoweringly hot, as though the earth's long, circular motion through space had been suspended, perhaps through a kind of cosmic lassitude, and that [sic] now the discouraged sphere was drifting slowly downwards through dense, sultry darkness toward a forced landing in the sun's great bin of ashes. No feeling of animation was in the air. Even the leaves of the peach tree, just outside the bedroom window, hung motionless like thousands of slender black fingers pointing with a curious insistence down at the earth. They seemed to indicate that something was buried down there, something that still lived and gasped for air. Its suffocation was palpable: he could feel it as plainly as he could his wife's deep, regular breathing.

"Uhhh, my God!" he muttered.

He sat up in bed. Hot rivulets of sweat coursed between the two points of his collar-bone. He tore the pajama coat open and drew a deep breath. It gave him no relief, there was no freshness in it. The curtains that hung at the window, the curtain of leaves beyond them, filled him with savage impatience. Too many walls, he thought, too many little partitions! The world is full of waste matter. He pushed the lace curtains aside and peered up at the sky. No stars were in sight, only a dull, impenetrable grey. The brilliant region of the heavens through which things moved with the rapturous precision of a dance, had now been lost completely, was left far above this thickening, dull atmosphere through which dead planets drifted. . . .

He turned and looked down at the sleeping body of his wife. She lay without moving. Her arms were flung wide across both pillows, unconsciously asserting even in sleep her full proprietorship. Her fingers were loosely curled. They made him think of those pale, moist flowers of the insectivorous kind. They looked as though some vegetable sentience in them would make them close on the unsuspecting intruder. Her face had a blank, empty look which did not reassure him but rather intensified the malignantly vegetative aspect her sleeping body had taken.

Without knowing why, he got quietly out of bed and began to dress.

"I want something cool," he muttered to himself as he moved toward the front of the house.

He pushed the screen door open. It was not altogether dark outside. The sky refracted a grey leaden light that was like the light in a subterranean vault, coming deviously through cob-webbed chinks. To the east was a very faint, nacreous blur back of which the moon was concealed. It was possible to see the shapes of houses across the street, the low peaked rooves of the monotonous brick bungalows and here and there the ambiguous shadow of a tree shape or dark line of a hedge. In his own yard he could see the black fountain of the crepe myrtle bush and the faint, faint whiteness of honeysuckle along the screens of the porch. The sweetness was cloyingly heavy, it thickened the air, so he moved away from it, down the walk from the steps and then to the left, along the street toward the park about two blocks beyond. Mechanically he lifted his watch from the pocket of his linen pants and stared down at it until the glow from a street-lamp made the dial visible to him. Eight after twelve was the time. "Good," he murmured without the slightest conviction. "A short walk will cool me off and then I can go home and sleep." But the thought of returning was still repugnant to him. He saw again the vacant, vegetative look of his sleeping wife's face and her curled fingers and he felt once more the nearly desperate need for some kind of coolness somewhere. . . .

At the end of the block was a drug-store but it was closed.

Cigarettes?

Yes, I still have some.

He thrust one in his mouth and struck a match. The lightless corner, whose lamp had been demolished some nights before when a car full of drunk adolescents plunged over the curb, now bloomed in wavering twilight. Windows and walls winked at him, the Chesterfield girl smiled dimly. And in this momentary flare he saw something white in the drug-store doorway. It stirred a little and uttered a low, sharp cry.

The match flickered out but its light had been long enough to establish the figure as that of a woman in white.

"Hello," he said quickly. He was surprised at the clear, relieved tone of his voice. Why should it please him so much to find a strange woman on this deserted street-corner?

For a second or two his greeting was left unanswered. Then the vague white shadow moved out of the doorway and glided noiselessly toward him.

"You frightened me," she murmured.

They both laughed a little uncertainly.

"Why?"

With her face half averted, she seemed for a moment to consider this question.

"I don't know. I'm terribly nervous," she told him. "You live on the block, don't you?"

"Yes."

"So do I. I have a terrible headache. I wanted to buy something for it but the drug-store's closed."

"It's after midnight."

"I know, I know, but I wasn't able to sleep!"

She lifted one hand to her forehead. Her face was lowered and half concealed by the broad white brim of her hat. He wondered what she looked like.

"Do you work?" he asked.

"Yes."

"That's bad. I'm in the same boat."

She laughed softly and without moving seemed to approach him still closer.

"Let's walk," he suggested.

"Oh, would you like to?" she answered eagerly. "I think that would help a lot. Just to be moving around makes a little coolness on your face, don't you think?"

They had already started across the street and were continuing up the next block toward the park.

"It's nice of you to walk with me. I'm afraid to walk by myself at night. You read so often about girls getting in trouble."

They were passing beneath a lamp post and he looked quickly down to probe the meaning of her speech. Was it a warning to him, or rather a bit of calculated suggestion? Her face was still hidden, however, beneath the white hat. His eyes dropped down to her figure and observed that it was youthfully slender with breasts firm and moderately full. It may have been only the effect of the white costume, but she seemed to emanate an atmosphere of coolness which he found very pleasant. I won't try to look at her more closely, he decided. Her face might turn out to be definitely unattractive and that would spoil it all. . . .

"Have a cigarette," he offered. She took one. They walked on in silence till they reached the end of the block. Across the street was the black domain of the park. This section was like a jungle. There was something forbidding, frightening about its utter blackness. It made you feel that to enter would be to lose yourself completely and forever, but at the same time it excited a perverse desire to enter and be lost. . . .

"Shall we cross?" he asked softly.

Her hesitation seemed to create a fluttering movement in the darkness around them.

"Shall we?" she echoed.

Such a suggestion of pliancy was held in her tone, that his last doubt left him. He laughed and caught at her elbow. She moved very lightly before him. Her skirt made a whispering sound. The sleeve of her blouse slid over his own white sleeve and its touch was as light as the brush of a cool white feather.

Gravel crunched under their feet.

"I can't see!" she breathed. "It's so pitch dark that I can't make out a thing!"

"Here! I'll guide you!" he whispered, catching hold of her hand. As he did so he felt a ring. There was no stone in it. The metal was broad and flat. A signet or class-ring he thought. She isn't married. . . .

After a moment his eyes were able to penetrate the deep grey before him and he picked out the black trail of a bridle-path winding among a maze of hedges and shrubbery into the interior of the park. As they moved along this path he looked sharply to right and left but could find no suitable place. It was all overgrown with bushes.

"Oh, I've been so nervous all week!" the girl exclaimed.

"Have you?" he answered absently, intent upon his search.

"Yes! I've felt so restless! Like I ought to be doing something but I don't know what!"

Her fingers pressed slightly into the cup of his palm.

This was superfluous, he thought. There was enough already to make them sure of each other.

"I guess it's the heat," she went on. "Hot weather always makes me restless—I'm from up North, you know."

"Oh, are you?"

"Yes, I thought you could tell by my voice."

"It is a little different."

For some reason he was pleased by the fact that she came from away. He didn't want to know from exactly where. The word "north" had a remote and unspecific charm. He thought vaguely of snow-mantled landscape and cool expanses of green water.

They had now gone past the zoo. The warm, fetid odor of the animal cages was left behind and they had reached the loveliest part of the park, the open space surrounding the Chinese lagoon, the golf-club and the refreshment pavilion. The links rose before them in a long, even swell of fragrant grass and on the top was silhouetted a row of giant trees against the grey sky. Benches were scattered here and there along the lake shore. The water was a level blackness.

They walked closer to its edge. Willow leaves brushed his forehead. To the left he saw the pagoda-shaped roof of the pavilion. The heat seemed to recede. There was no wind stirring and yet a coolness passed over his body. He felt his fingers spasmodically tightening upon the girl's hand. Dark, glittering wings were lifted inside him and their tumultuous motion filled the night.

The girl was the first to speak. Her voice was nearly stifled.

"Let's stay here a minute."

"Yes, let's do," he answered. "Let's sit down on the grass!"

"Is it dry?"

Once more he felt that breathless hesitancy in her voice.

"Perfectly," he assured her.

For a moment her fingers slightly resisted the pull of his hand. Then she seated herself beside him.

"This is a crazy thing to be doing," she said. "Wouldn't it give my boss a laugh if he could see me doing a crazy thing like this?"

"Your boss!" he scoffed impatiently. "What business is it of his?"

She suddenly jerked her hand from his and leaned slightly away from him.

"I'm in *love* with my boss," she whispered.

Instantly the adventure's whole aspect was changed. The mysterious wings in the air about him grew still and the heat seemed to settle again. The hot, turgid presence of human relations hovered about him once more and he felt an unreasonably strong resentment.

"What kind of a stall is this?" he muttered.

"What do you mean, a stall?"

"What is it then? We take a walk, we come to a nice cool place, there seems to be a kind of understanding, and then all at once, like a silly jack-out-of-the box, your boss sticks his head in between us!"

"The head of my boss!"

She spent her breath in a fit of violent laughter.

"The head of my boss," she repeated, "the head of my boss."

"What's funny about it?"

Her laughter stopped short, her breath was caught in a sob.

"He *does* have a head," she said.

"I'm sure that he does. In fact I can see it plainly. It's rather bald and puffy-looking. Resembling nothing so much as a slightly green tomato."

"Oh, no!" she breathed. "That isn't *his* description!"

Her tone was so shocked that it amused him.

"What does he look like then?"

"He looks very much like *you!*"

"Me? "

His interest was stimulated once more. The situation had narrowed a moment before to only include the strange young woman in white and her alleged employer. But now its bounds expanded around himself again and he felt more at ease.

"How can you tell what I look like in this darkness?"

"I couldn't *now*. But I saw your face when you struck the match on the corner."

"Oh. And I look like your boss?"

"Surprisingly much. That's why I cried out loud when I saw your face in the match-light!"

"So that was the reason?"

"Yes—I actually thought you were *him!*"

"How absurd!"

"Yes, it *was* absurd. That's the terrible thing about it," she whispered. "If love could be dignified, it wouldn't be so awful, would it?"

"Isn't it dignified?"

"No, not for me. It makes me act like a fool."

She raised a dab of white to her invisible face and made a faint, sniffling sound.

"Nothing much ever happened to me before this," she whispered. "I went to business-school. Economized on lunches at the drug-store so I could go to a show once a week. Sunday I wrote home to my mother in Webb, Mississippi. I never had much to say. It was hard to fill two pages about business-school. I told her the scores I made in the latest typing drills and what my Gregg speed was. And she was pretty satisfied with that. She seemed to be sure that I would manage to get a good job some day. And it turned out that I did. This man's stenographer quit and he needed another and I saw the ad in the paper and when I applied for the job, he didn't even look at me, just asked what my typing speed was and gave me a little dictation and told me to start work Monday. I had on a light pink dress and when I got up, he asked me not to wear pink. I've got an allergy to pink, he said. That's the only personal thing he's ever said to me. And just the other day I wore the pink dress again because I thought it might make him look at me and make some personal remark. But he didn't. He just frowned a little when I walked in the office. He wears a white linen suit most days in summer, with a pale blue tie. Maybe when I have on pink it looks too much like it was a social occasion. You guess that's it?—I don't know. At first I only thought to myself *He's nice!*—And that's all it was. It started out very slowly, the way that some fevers start, hardly noticeable, a fraction of a degree one day, another fraction the next, till all of a sudden you find that you're burning up, your flesh is on fire, your bones nearly *melted* with it!"

"Is that how it is?"

"Yes!—I always felt that I had a big empty space in me, a kind of a room, without any furniture in it. I used to wonder what that emptiness was and why it was there. And then one day I happened to go by the door and the room was full, it was completely furnished!—You see what I mean?—But I couldn't go inside!"

"Why not?"

"The air was *solid* against me, it wouldn't let me in."

"Is that how it is?"

"Exactly!"

Love, he thought. Love . . .

A curious sickness!

"If I could cry out," she went on, "If I could *scream*—if I could make a big scene—that might be some relief. But I can't or I'd lose my job! I have to walk back and forth, back and forth, with bunches of legal papers, open drawers, shut drawers, bang away at those goddam little white keys!—Sometimes I want to stop and say to him, very quietly, 'This is against my nature!'—D'you guess he'd understand?"

"He might."

"I don't think so."

She tossed her head far back.

"He would say—'You are not satisfied?'—And if I said 'No!' he would think that I meant with the *job!*"

"If he isn't a fool he's probably noticed something."

"No. He's blind with something himself the same as I am."

"What's *he* blind with?"

"With love."

"With *love?*"

"Yes, of course. What else could it be?—I hear them talk on the 'phone and when he hangs up, his head bends over the desk, I can see the little pink lines where his scalp shows through his hair, and once he was holding a pencil that snapped in two!"

"Hmmm."

"You see how fantastic it is?"

"Yes."

"If something could be very straight, very simple, very white and cool-looking, what a relief it would be!"

"Um-hmm. I see what you mean."

"But nothing's like that. It's all tangled up and confused and the heat is something terrific!"

"Yes."

"I went to the priest and said, 'Father, I've got to have peace!'"

"Did he give you peace?"

"No, of course not! How could he?"

"Hmmm."

"What can I do?"

"I don't know."

"No. There is nothing. The situation is hopeless."

"I wouldn't say that.—How does your boss feel about *you?*"

"He *despises* me!" she said quickly. "He thinks that I'm silly! Yesterday when he asked me to take a letter I started crying. I couldn't help myself. He asked me what was the matter and I told him I guessed it must be the heat."

A note of strangled laughter shook from her throat.

"Can't you snap out of it?"

"No, I *can't!*" she sobbed. "I've tried so *hard!*"

For a minute neither of them spoke. A dim white shape was moving in from the center of the lake. There was something spectral about its quiet, leisurely approach. It made a barely distinguishable rippling sound as it moved.

With a low gasp the girl rose and caught at his arm.

"Oh, my, what is *that?*"

"A swan," he answered. The sound of the word gave him a quick pleasure. It diverted him from the girl's unhappy problem. He turned away from her shadowy whiteness to the more distant and still more shadowy whiteness of the floating bird.

"A swan? Why, yes, so it *is!*"

There was a note of sudden eagerness in her voice. She crouched toward the water's edge and coaxingly held out one hand toward the spectral white bird but it only stared at her from a casual distance upon the level black surface of the water and then wheeled about, like a sailboat catching fresh wind, and floated silently off till its white shape faded and diminished into the Stygian blackness from which it had come.

When the girl leaned back, sighing a little, her shoulder touched his. He had almost forgotten her presence as he watched the withdrawing swan, but now he suddenly remembered her and the touch of her shoulder released some inner violence and he flung his arm roughly about her and pressed her down toward the grass.

"Don't!" she breathed. But made no move to resist. He was shocked at the violence of his action. It was more like an act of fury than an act of love. Dimly he realized, in the unenflamed areas of his mind, that it was not the girl that he was possessing. It was the cool, white, unpossessable purity of the swan.

Her lips were stammering something against his.

"Daniel, Daniel!" she whispered.

He wondered vaguely whose name it was—and in an instant her arms flew around him and her fingers clawed wildly at his shoulders.

"Daniel, Daniel!"

The cry still made him wonder until at the moment when every thought is extinguished, it came to him in a burning wave of compassion that this was the name of her boss—and was now *his* name as *hers* had become *the swan!*

* * *

They walked in silence. Separate. Cool. Relaxed.

"How is your headache?" he asked her as they went by the drug-store corner where he had met her an hour before.

"It's all gone now," she murmured.

"So's mine. I guess we'll be able to sleep the rest of the night."

"I hope so," she murmured. "Well, here's my place."

He looked toward the dark shape of the old-fashioned red brick boarding house. And as he looked at it he suddenly saw also the face of the girl in full daylight. He saw her getting off at his car-stop in the evenings and walking a little distance in front of him up the block to this house. He saw a face shining with perspiration and colorless except for a sunburned nose. He saw a chin that was slightly recessive and glittering rimless glasses and black hair that straggled beneath a shapeless white felt hat. It was a very plain face, a face which, in full daylight, he would never have given a second glance.

"Good night," he said quickly. He started moving away and he felt the girl standing motionless, watching him, and after a painfully long interval, he heard her own footsteps recommencing, going slowly up the walk and then up the steps of the red brick boarding house.

Then he remembered the swan moving in from the center of the lake, the white, wing-like rustling of the girl's linen skirt as she walked beside him, and the feeling of coolness returned, the memory (image?) of her face was forgotten.

There was only the smooth black lake and the swan.

Tennessee Williams
Memphis
September 1939

© 2003 Jen Sorensen

www.slowpokecomics.com

TOBIAS WOLFF

© Giliola Christe

Tobias Wolff's short stories have appeared in magazines such as *The New Yorker*, *Esquire* and *Atlantic Monthly* and have been collected in three books—*In the Garden of the North American Martyrs* (1981), *Back in the World* (1985), and *The Night in Question* (1996). He received the PEN/Faulkner Award for his 1984 novella *The Barracks Thief*, and his two memoirs, *This Boy's Life* (1989) and *In Pharaoh's Army: Memories of the Lost War* enjoyed similar success. *This Boy's Life* was turned into a movie in 1993, and *In Pharaoh's Army* was a finalist for the National Book Award in 1994.

A former newspaper reporter, **William Bradley** is now a graduate student and creative nonfiction writer at the University of Missouri.

An Interview with Tobias Wolff/*William Bradley*

Interviewer: In your new novel, *Old School*, your narrator claims—truthfully, it seems to me—"No true account can be given of how or why you became a writer. . . ." However, I wonder if you could tell me a little bit about the course of events that led you to pursue a career as a writer.

Wolff: It was, I suppose, a tendency in my nature, to some extent encouraged by my reading, and at one point by the example of my brother, Geoffrey, who is seven and a half years older than I. When a brother is that far ahead of you, he has a kind of avuncular influence because you don't compete with him the way you would with a brother who's closer to your age. Although we grew up on opposite ends of the country, when I was about fifteen we spent a summer together. He had just graduated from college and was absolutely book-drunk. He'd been an English major and wanted to be a writer himself. He had me reading all kinds of writers I'd never even known existed—Sophocles, Camus, you name it. That was a crucially important summer for me. I hadn't seen Geoffrey in six years. It was like meeting someone new and dazzling, who was at the same time my brother. I looked up to him, and his enthusiasms were catching.

Interviewer: Was that what awakened your interest in writing?

Wolff: Even as a boy I'd written stories. I never stopped writing them. I used to write them for friends of mine, to turn in for extra credit. Of course they were childish, imitative things, like any kid writes, but I loved writing, and I loved reading. I never really made the connection between the things I read and the writing I was doing until I was a freshman in high school, when a friend of mine said to me one day, "You should be a writer," and the idea stuck. Though I read a lot and loved to write, it had never occurred to me to be a writer, but somehow that suggestion, coming from a fourteen-year-old boy, forced a connection between those two passions. I thought, "Huh. I could be a writer. I write, I read."

But you can't trace this vocation or any other to a single event or set of circumstances. It's really the way life plays on your temperament, on your interests—which of course change from time to time. And—this is something people don't say very much about—it has a lot to do with what you're *not* good at. After a while your choices get winnowed down by your inabilities as much as they're formed by your abilities. There are one hell of a lot of things I can't do. So I do what I can, like anyone else.

Interviewer: In *This Boy's Life*, you say that you sent a story to your brother about two dogs fighting in the wilderness, and in the collection *For the Love of Books*, which Ronald B. Schwartz edited, you talk about how, as a child, you were attracted to those stories of animals in the wild. Although you might not have been aware of them at the time, do you recognize distinct stages in your writing now, correlating to what you were reading at the time?

Wolff: The stories that you mentioned were written under the influence of Jack London. Later I fell under the spell of Hemingway, or Hemingway as I perceived him then—his stories look to a young teenage boy like something he can write too. I couldn't understand the experience and the depth of artistry that went into his stories, but it looked easy. I did a lot of that kind of imitation. I learned by imitating—and that's fine. People don't appreciate the extent to which writers need to imitate in order to get where they're going, or how long the apprenticeship will be. When we go to a concert and hear how effortlessly Wynton Marsalis plays the trumpet, we don't go home afterward and think we can do that too. But when we read Hemingway, we're apt to think, "Well, hell, I know all those words. I can put them in that order. I could be Hemingway." Writing is one art where people fool themselves into thinking it's easier than it is.

Interviewer: In *Old School*, you address imitation, and imitation when it goes too far and becomes plagiarism. In the novel, the incident is presented in such a way that the audience does not necessarily feel obligated to condemn the plagiarist. I was wondering about your own thoughts regarding plagiarism?

Wolff: That's a good question. In all honesty, at first blush it's rather flattering to be plagiarized. And the plagiarist has already been punished;

"You can't trace this vocation or any other to a single event. . . . It's really the way life plays on your temperament."

---

the very act of plagiarizing means that you have confessed an inability to do something on your own, which is a pretty harsh verdict to bring on yourself. No one else can condemn you more than you have already condemned yourself. So there's something pathetic about the plagiarist.

But there are distinctions to be made. There's the sort of plagiarist who does it strictly for reasons of personal advantage at school or work. This is the dullest and most contemptible kind, and a very different thing from plagiarism of a creative work, which usually proceeds, paradoxically, from admiration.

Interviewer: How is that kind different, in your mind?

Wolff: It's often a very good, passionate reader who plagiarizes a story—someone whose connection with a given work becomes so powerful that his sense of it being "his" story—a feeling every writer wants to create in the reader—allows him to forget that he did not, in fact, create the story. But think of it. A story—a written story—is a series of black marks on a white page. That's it. And from these marks the reader is conjuring up Anna and her love for Vronsky, or the retreat from Caporetto. Readers share in the active imagination of these worlds, and this forges an intimacy between the reader and the writer. In the intensity of their reactions, some readers will cross the line and confuse themselves with the writer. Say the writer is revealing something that seems straight from your own soul, your own life—that you feel belongs to you. You might then convince yourself that the plagiarism you're committing is actually personal revelation. It can even seem an act of honest confession.

It's no accident that the man who shot Jesse James, Robert Ford, revered Jesse James and sometimes went by his name. The man who shot John Lennon, Mark David Chapman, used to check in to hotels under the name John Lennon. He admired Lennon so much, took his music so *personally*, that he lost his sense of where one ended and the

"You're always lagging behind your best ideas. Your in-house critic has always got the jump on you."

other began. He had to subsume the other by killing him. Plagiarism is a sort of psychological annihilation and appropriation of the other. It's very atavistic, in a way. It's like eating someone's brain or their heart to take on their qualities.

There's a very interesting case from the late nineteenth century of a novelist who wrote a novel called *Olympia* that chronicled the affairs of a society woman. A young man in Philadelphia became convinced that the woman in the novel was his sister and that therefore the novelist had slandered her. Well, there was no actual connection at all between the novelist, who lived in New York, and this man's sister, who also lived in Philadelphia. But there was something in the novel that was so persuasive to this young man that he began to stalk the novelist and eventually shot him dead.

It was the same impulse at work that I think the plagiarist feels: that this somehow belongs to you and you're taking what's yours. That may be an odd way of coming at it, but I think there's something there. Again, I'm not talking about the guy who's doing it for a grade in a class or to advance his career at *The New Republic*. That's a different thing altogether. But there is a kind of plagiarist who defies easy definition, who participates, however perversely, in the creative life of the writer.

Interviewer: As you began your writing career, did you have many disappointments?

Wolff: Well, yes—mainly disappointments in myself. You have an idea in mind of what you want to achieve when you sit down to write something. It takes many years to accept that you will always fall short of that. Maybe now I can write the book that I might have had in mind five or twenty years ago. You're always lagging behind your best ideas. Your in-house critic has always got the jump on you. That's good insofar as it sets a standard, forces you to stretch and grow, but at the same time there's always that wince at falling a little short. Now and then you might get away with something, and even the critic in you will say, "Well done." But most of the time, it's, "Hmm, pretty good, but . . ."

Interviewer: Does it get easier or harder?

Wolff: The only thing that gets easier about it is at least you know you can do it. You finish a good number of stories in your life, and you've written a few books; then you know that if you stay with it, it'll get done. You don't know that when you first start out. It does seem, sometimes, endless, and you wonder if you have the stuff to finish a book, to really bring a good story home. After a while you learn that if you stay with it you'll get there. In that sense it gets easier.

But the work itself? No, because you're always asking more of yourself. In that way, no, it doesn't get easier. I wouldn't say it gets harder, though.

Interviewer: Do you set any schedule or minimum time limit when you sit down to work, or do you allow yourself more flexibility?

Wolff: When I'm generating a story or a book to begin with, I tend to work a little less than when I'm revising. Once I get something finished and I start the process of revision, I work fairly long hours at it. I find that very exciting. The other is a little more difficult and draining. You know, I have three children, and I teach and do other things. So I can't pretend to keep absolute banker's hours at my writing desk, though I wish I could. That's just not possible in real life.

Interviewer: Is there any pressure to live up to what you've done in the past? When a book is as well received as *This Boy's Life*, or three stories from one collection are chosen for *Best American?*

Wolff: Sure. You don't want to be worse than your last book. If you've had a book that's done well, you want your next book to do at least as well. But you also know that you can't really gauge the quality of a book by its reception. Most of the books on the best-seller list, for example, even those of the supposedly literary caste, don't generally bowl me over. So I'm not going to beat myself up for not being on it. I consider it a wonderful piece of luck if a book gets a warm reception and sells a lot of copies. Obviously one wants that to happen, but it isn't the standard by which I judge my own or anyone else's work.

Interviewer: Can you speak a little about the standards by which you do judge your work?

Wolff: It's a very personal thing. I ask myself, "Would I be interested in reading this? Would this speak to me?" If the answer is no, then this is not a work that I would want to wish on anyone else. It isn't that I don't care whether other people like my work or not—I do—but I can't second-guess other readers. I don't know what other readers like or don't like, and I can't try to tailor my writing to a bunch of phantoms. The only person whose tastes I'm absolutely certain of are my own. I know what I like, and it isn't something that satisfies a particular theory of writing or life; it's just in the writing itself and in the moment-by-moment progress of a story or a book that I find pleasure or interest in. That's the standard, finally, that I hold myself to: whether or not I would finish the damn thing if I were the reader.

Interviewer: Toward the end of *Old School*, the narrator meditates on the writer's life and concludes that it's not really as solitary as others make it out to be. He compares the writer to a monk in a cell, praying for the world, a task "performed alone, but for other people."

Wolff: That's him at a certain age. That probably wouldn't be my last word on it, or his.

Interviewer: You do hear about writers lamenting—with various degrees of seriousness—that so much of the writer's life is spent alone, gazing inward. Is that a concern for you?

Wolff: It certainly is. There is a sort of healthy detachment, I think, but to be habitually isolated and removed from life can encourage a selfishness that will be no good to you as a person or as a writer: a selfishness about the sanctity of your time and privacy. I think it would be very much to the benefit of a lot of writers to be thrown out into the world a little more. William Butler Yeats's father once said, "Writing is the social act of a solitary man." There is a sense in which you're most social when you're most alone as a writer because you're addressing other people and creating a community of readers. You hope you are, anyway. But I would be lying if I said this very privileged life didn't have some traps for the soul.

Interviewer: In 1984 you received the PEN/Faulkner award for *The Barracks Thief*. Since then, the works we've seen from you have been

"I would be lying if I said this very privileged life didn't have some traps for the soul."

memoirs and short stories. What's motivated your return to longer fiction now?

Wolff: This was the story I wanted to tell, and it ended up being this long. It's just as simple as that. I had originally conceived it as a long story. Robert Frost visited my school when I was a boy, and I'd been thinking about that. Then I remembered this literary competition we used to have, and that found its way in. Then there were two other writers. The story grew into a novel; I didn't sit down and say, "I'm going to write a novel." It grew under my hand as I was writing. It was longer than it is now; I've done quite a bit of trimming, as I tend to do when I'm revising. It wasn't a strategic decision: "Okay, I've written two memoirs and three collections of short stories. Time for a novel." That's not what happened.

Interviewer: As someone who writes both nonfiction and fiction that often comes from your own experiences, are you concerned that readers might read your autobiographical fiction and make assumptions about your life?

Wolff: I'm afraid that's not something I can avoid, especially if I go into the first person. That's something I have to live with; I don't know what I can do about it at this point. I have written a couple of memoirs, and it would be preposterous of me to insist that readers divorce themselves from all memory of anything else I've written when approaching something new.

I do take the distinction between genres very seriously. When I call something a memoir, it's my understanding with the readers that they can accept this story as a chronicle of actual events as I remember them. When I call something a novel, it's fiction, and readers need to be smart about that. You don't want to pick up a novel and assume that it's true. If it were, the writer would call it a memoir instead.

"Good writers are often . . . better than their intentions."

But I can't stop readers from reading the way they're going to read. I know that certain stories of mine have invited autobiographical readings because they seem to coincide with my memoirs. People have said to me, "Why didn't you include, say, 'Firelight' in *This Boy's Life*?" and the answer to that is, "Because it didn't happen." I might use colors from the same palette and use experiences from my memory and my own life, but I take off. I'm not loyal to the facts or to my memory. I'm really inventing. I'm after a different kind of truth, if you will, when I write fiction.

There's no question at all, though, that the genres cross. Readers understandably might wonder if such-and-such a thing happened. There are elements of *Old School* that are autobiographical, no question about it. The competition among aspiring writers at my old school is something I've often thought about and wanted to get down: the love of literature that would now seem almost miraculous among kids that young; the presence of luminary writers at our school from time to time, and how those visits stoked our own hopes and fantasies. I wanted to try to capture that. How considerations of class confused that passage of my life, encouraging in me a tendency to pretense. This was the first real encounter I had with the power of class to determine destiny.

So a lot of things went into the writing of this book that came, if not out of my direct experience, then from the experience of my spirit when I was growing up. All that played a part. However, if you consider the events in this book against a historical standard, it's very much a novel.

Interviewer: Like many other writers, you don't really like to talk about what you've written—at least not in much detail.

Wolff: I don't know what I would say about it. I don't want to dictate to the reader how to read my work. It's anybody's to interpret; I don't have control over it, and I don't like shutting down the possibility of readers coming to their own conclusions by telling them to see it this way or that way. It is what it is; it's on the page, and readers will make of it what they will. I kind of like the play of possibilities that readers bring to a work, sometimes noticing things that, in all honesty, I hadn't really intended but were actually there. That is, they were not at the conscious level of intention, and yet they were demonstrably part of the work. Good writers are often if not generally better than their intentions. What makes writing so interesting is all the unexpected things that happen when you write. If you write according to a blueprint and it comes out just the way you designed it, my guess is that it's not going to be very interesting work. Not very lively. The best work I do comes out of the ways in which I'm surprised while I'm writing, out of the ways that the original notion of the story or the book gets waylaid by promptings I couldn't anticipate.

Wallace Stevens once said, "No surprise for the writer, no surprise for the reader." That's just what I'm talking about here. You are subject to all kinds of confrontations with unexpected material and revelations when you write. If you weren't, you would hardly want to do it. It would just be typewriting, as Truman Capote would say; it wouldn't be writing. The process of writing is made exciting by these moments.

Interviewer: Do you ever find yourself torn when deciding whether to make something a work of nonfiction or fiction? Or by the time you get to the writing stage is it pretty clear in your mind?

Wolff: *Old School* was clearly going to be fiction. I never had any hesitation about how to frame this particular book. I was hesitant with writing *This Boy's Life*, at the beginning. It had never crossed my mind before I started it to write a memoir. It overwhelmed me, really; it took me by surprise that that's what I was, in fact, doing. In the initial stages I would, from time to time, try to pull it off course and start fictionalizing it. It just didn't work at all when I did that, So I finally had to be clear with myself because a memoir and a novel are very different. They may not appear so to the reader, but to the writer they are fundamentally, organically *different*. You can't fudge it. You have to know what you're doing; you have to be very clear about it.

But I do understand that that difference is not always clear to readers. Bookstores sometimes put *This Boy's Life* in the novel section, and readers have said, "Oh, this would be a good novel. Why didn't you just call it a novel?" I didn't call it a novel because it's a memoir. I couldn't have written it as I did if I had conceived of it as a novel. The truth of it is, I don't think it would be a good novel. It's not supposed to be read as a novel, and if it were, I don't think it would be successful. It's not shaped that way. No novel could acceptably end as this book does. It's too open, as a life is open. It would have been false to bring it to the kind of conclusiveness we expect in a novel. I know that some readers are really frustrated by the ending. "Okay, well, how did you end up writing the book then? How did you get from there to here?" I had hoped that the reader would understand even by the title *This Boy's Life* that when the kid is no longer a boy, when that parental safety net is gone and he's on his own, this particular story is over. He's launched into the world, and that's the end of that boy's life. He's not a boy anymore.

Also, I encounter questions as to how or why the boy in this book became a writer. People say, "There's no clue given." Well, I think there is. This is somebody who's inventing himself constantly and who is aware of stories and books and the power of stories to create another reality. These are things I discovered about myself in writing the book. I'd forgotten the way I used to change my name all the time, whenever we would move. When I started writing the book I remembered that. Indeed, when I go back to Washington State and see people I went to high school with there, they still call me Jack. That's their name for me. But when I started writing it, I hadn't talked to anybody who called me Jack in twenty-five years. I'd forgotten.

And it was amazing how much I had not truly forgotten but had not thought of for many years that came out in the writing. I had to cut so much stuff it was unbelievable. People said, "How do you remember so much?" My God, I remembered ten times what I had in there. The problem was finding the patterns by which to organize the book and give it a structure that would reflect the arc of the life, while at the same time not repeat things constantly—which meant a great deal of excision.

Interviewer: Is there an impulse, sometimes, to fictionalize what really happened in an effort to protect someone?

Wolff: I changed names. That was my device for protecting people. It didn't seem to work very well, since everybody knew who everyone else was. I mean, those who would know, knew. I wouldn't say there was an impulse to "fictionalize." You have to emphasize and ignore certain things in order to create a narrative at all. You're shaping constantly. Even putting experience into language is to shape it, put your stamp on it. This is not an innocent activity, right? I mean, it's got consequences. You're making it personal. That's why people's memories of the same thing are different. So you get this natural shaping that to another person might seem to be fictionalizing. But having said that,

"This is not an innocent activity, right? I mean, it's got consequences."

I also have to say that the people I went through these experiences with were all alive and they were certainly aware of the books. They were going to read them. If my own honesty weren't enough, there's a built-in discipline from the knowledge that I've got people reading over my shoulder who know very well what happened, and that definitely discourages one from being too exuberantly imaginative.

Interviewer: Yet memory is still subjective.

Wolff: All accounts of the past are subjective. I remember a piece that William H. Gass wrote about ten years ago, called "Autobiography in the Age of Narcissim," in which he pretty much dismissed all memoir and autobiography as an illegitimate form of literature. He even has a sentence in there: "He who writes his memoirs is already a monster." His argument is that it's a bastard branch of history, but without the documentary spine, so to speak, without the objectivity and detachment of history, the commitment to reach the truth. That autobiography and memoir are too inevitably self-serving to satisfy the standards either of literature or history.

Interestingly enough, he doesn't mention a single memoir in his essay. Like all Gass's work, the essay is very smart and beautifully written, but it's fundamentally wrong. I think the reason he doesn't mention a single book is because once he opens that gate he loses his whole thesis. Who would dispute the achievement of Nabokov in *Speak Memory*, for example? Of Mary McCarthy in *Memories of a Catholic Girlhood?* Of my own brother Geoffrey in *The Duke of Deception?* I could go on citing memoirs that have succeeded to the status of literature, that are clearly not simply self-serving. That's not what their aim is, and certainly not their result.

But Gass's fundamental confusion, it seems to me, in his critique of the memoir form with reference to history, is the assumption that

"I can think of no better way to learn to appreciate the complexity and infinite possibilities of literature than to try to write some yourself."

---

historians are objective and detached and free of the imaginative, subjective impulse. If that were the case, all histories working from the same set of documents would reach the same conclusions, and of course they don't.

Interviewer: Speaking about history, much of your work is grounded in a specific time. You often write about America or Americans in the 1960s. Does that time in America's past hold a certain appeal for you?

Wolff: It must, because I have gone back to it. In this last book, when I started writing about the boys at this school, I felt as if I was writing about one of those tribes they discover now and then that still uses stone implements, you know? The moment they're discovered, everything's going to change; they'll have a satellite dish in their yard in two years.

That world I'm writing about is so close to us in years, and yet remote. It belongs as much to the nineteenth century as to its own time, 1961. There is that sense of having observed and having indeed even been part of a vanished culture that intrigued me. Part of that vanished culture wasn't just social; it was literary as well. I wanted to capture the moment just after Kennedy was elected, when Robert Frost was the poet supreme, Ayn Rand was building a really weird cult following and Hemingway set the pattern for young men—taught them not only how to write but how to talk and think and thirst for conflict in which to prove themselves. Well, we found it, and how. This was a particular moment in our national life, still rooted in an archaic past just before the convulsive transformations that we're still trying to make sense of. There are no black students in this school, for example. It's still a time when a headmaster would meet fierce opposition to bringing black, or rather Negro, students in. Such resistance would be unthinkable now at such a school; indeed they recruit black students—and it's only forty years later. That's no time at all in this world.

Interviewer: You bring up Robert Frost and Ayn Rand, and both of those authors, along with Hemingway, make appearances in the new book. Each is an influence on your narrator to varying degrees, but there's a sense that the narrator goes from adoration to questioning. Have you felt this same sense of connection and then questioning of your own influences?

Wolff: I wanted to capture the youthful conviction that whatever you're most passionate about that day has to be the greatest thing that's ever happened. So I wasn't really after an objective evaluation of these writers. They are as they are seen by a young acolyte, who, as time goes on, will see the flaws in one and proceed to another. This is a narrator in search of a father, and a god. He's looking for some kind of anointing; he wants something to transform him. He's looking for this in literature. But literature's a pretty tough god to follow.

The book takes the form of an homage to the power of literature, and to the writers who create it. But it isn't meant to be an act of hero worship. It simply records the power of influence, and the kinds of hopes that people pin on these dreams of transformation.

Interviewer: You teach one undergraduate creative writing class a year at Stanford. My understanding, though, is that you don't feel that writing can be taught.

Wolff: I don't think that anyone can be taught to be a writer. Absolutely not. And you never know who is going to be a writer. You don't know how people will develop. What you can do is help people become good editors of their own work. Even if, finally, the stories they write for you are not especially good, they will have learned something of what a writer thinks about, the kinds of questions and problems that a writer comes up against in achieving a piece of fiction. Even if they don't become writers—and very few will—they can become really good readers. I can think of no better way, in fact, to learn to appreciate the complexity and infinite possibilities of literature than to try to write some yourself.

Interviewer: What about the ones who do become writers? How, if at all, does your teaching influence them?

Wolff: Out of the hundreds of people one teaches over the course of a lifetime, some of them do it. Many of my students have become writers, some of them very successful writers. It wasn't because of me, but I was probably of help; maybe some of what they learned in my class helped them think about their work in a new and fruitful way. They don't write beautifully or interestingly because of me, but they may have gotten to where they wanted to go a little faster because of some of the things they learned. But you can't turn another person into a writer. It doesn't work that way.

Interviewer: A lot of writers give up teaching once they have achieved a certain level of success, but you've continued to teach. What's the appeal?

Wolff: You know, I could give it up. We could manage. But I would find it hard not to teach. If I'm doing too much of it, teaching eats into my work and I resent it, but I'm not doing so much that it really gets in the way. I'm teaching right now, for example, a lecture course with another professor here. The course meets twice a week, and we each lecture once a week. This is not terribly onerous. We've got two hundred freshmen, and we're teaching books we love. Two days ago, I gave an hour's lecture on Tolstoy's "The Death of Ivan Ilych," a very important story. Two-thirds of these young people are going to go into the sciences, in one way or another—medicine, computers, physics. They're not going to be humanists, at least not by occupation. This is a chance to help them frame questions about themselves, to help them learn the habit of questioning what they do, how they're spending their lives. And there's no better story for raising these questions than "Ivan Ilych."

I feel like I'm doing something in the world that's a good thing to do, when I'm doing that. I would miss it. I'd rattle around a bit too much if I didn't teach at all. I love my colleagues here, both the writers and my other friends in the university.

It's a community. Writers are isolated—we're scattered all over the country. We don't tend to have the writing colonies I think we used to have in New York or Chicago or San Francisco. It's a much more diffuse culture now, the literary culture of this country. So we make it where we are.

DIABLO/*Eric Puchner*

O FELIO CAMPOS STOOD at the edge of the eleventh floor, dreaming of beds. He thought of showroom floors and king-sized mattresses. He thought of sultanish waterbeds spotted like leopards. He thought of pillows. He thought of freshly washed sheets, crisp from the dryer, of a comforter he once slept under in a Las Vegas motel, folding him in like the wings of a bird.

Yawning, he looked through the empty window frame near his feet, peering down at the dump truck parked eleven floors below. The height made Ofelio's head swim. He held the piece of Sheetrock in his hand, nervously, trying to factor the persistent breeze into his throw. Every two weeks the construction crew finished a floor of the building and ascended to the next one, leaving a wake of rubble for him to remove. Ofelio pictured the crew like souls in purgatory, completing their penance so they could rise to the next level. At first, on the lower floors, he'd had to heave the rubble as hard as he could just to reach his target. Now, if Ofelio exerted any strength at all, whatever he was throwing flew too far and overshot its mark, exploding against the back wall of the dump trailer. It was impossible work, like trying to thread a needle in boxing gloves. The breeze made it especially difficult. Strips of drywall strayed from their target and broke over the side of the trailer into a million pieces.

Ofelio's muscles ached, a dull pain radiating from his shoulders and throbbing downward through his limbs. He closed his eyes for a second and dreamed of leaping from the window, of drifting soundlessly through the air—a weightless slumber—before landing in the dump truck among the studs and debris. What did he care about meeting God? The *cabrón* had done him no favors. Ofelio would sleep there in his bed of rubble, a lost soul, while the crew toiled upward.

He hadn't had a good night's sleep for years. Five, six hours at the most. In letters, describing America to his family, he said: *They have the most beautiful beds in the world, but they never use them.*

Ofelio gripped the large piece of Sheetrock and held it carefully over the edge. He aimed it at the truck bed, nudging gently to the left to compensate for the breeze. The Sheetrock fell through the air without spinning. For a moment, it seemed like a perfect shot. But then it drifted from its mark and landed with a loud smack on the top of the cab, breaking into smoky fragments and making a large crater in the roof. He squeezed his eyes shut again, just for a second, but it didn't undo the damage. From where he stood, the white pieces remaining on the cab looked like an unfinished jigsaw puzzle.

"Fuck!" yelled Mr. Kitchens, who'd joined Ofelio at the edge of the window frame. "Can't you aim worth shit?"

"I aimed, but the wind steal it."

"That's an International, Campos! Not a fucking Tonka toy!"

"The truck is very small. Look. Maybe this is not the intelligent way to remove trash."

"Intelligent way. Let me ask you then, Stephen J. Hawking. Do you have any idea what that truck costs?"

Ofelio shook his head.

"You could work the rest of your life for me," Mr. Kitchens said sternly, "and not earn enough for that truck." This sounded, to Ofelio, like a profound truth. Mr. Kitchens took off his hard hat and spat into the rubble at his feet. His face was perpetually sunburned, so that the blondness of his mustache seemed strange and out of place, like something blown onto his lip. "I'll tell you something intelligent, Campos. Watching you work is like watching a monkey fuck a football."

Ofelio followed Mr. Kitchens to the doorless freight elevator, supposing that he was meant to accompany him. He'd lived here three years already, but Mr. Kitchens's English still managed to surprise him. If his boss wasn't yelling at the crew, he was talking about Wife's Pussy. "Wife's Pussy tastes like banana cream pie," he'd say at lunch. Or: "I'll tell you something about fresh. Wife's Pussy has no preservatives. None of this Cool Whip shit." Or: "I didn't think Wife's Pussy could get any fresher, but last night she topped it all. Like sorbet, right? I was going down there to clean my palate." In Mexico, of course, there was much talk about pussies, but people would never discuss their wives' unless they were medically concerned about something. Once, in downtown San Francisco, Ofelio had run into his boss by accident; he'd been walking down the sidewalk with an overweight woman in a Rolling Stones T-shirt, who was scolding him in a teacherly voice. Ofelio had been about to wave, but something in Mr. Kitchens's face— a quaint and boyish misery—told him not to announce his presence.

Ofelio stepped outside into the bulldozed lot, still trailing Mr. Kitchens. With a feeling of helplessness, he rounded the hood of the dump truck to see for himself: a large fern of cracks spanned the entire width of the windshield. Mr. Kitchens sighed theatrically, as if to control his temper. "Take the rest of the day off, Campos," he said, glancing at his watch. "Try out for the Giants with that aim of yours. If you don't make the team, we'll see you tomorrow."

The construction site was in Alameda, an hour and a half by bus and BART from his apartment in the Mission District, which meant getting up at four-thirty in the morning so he could be on the train before dawn. The commute was bad enough, but he never seemed to make enough money to relax even for a minute. Of the $1,800 he earned every month, Ofelio sent nine hundred home to his wife and two children in Oaxaca. The monthly wire transfers allowed them to pay their mortgage on the house, a brand new *casita* he'd bought when he'd owned a transmission repair shop, before the business had gone bankrupt and saddled him with debts. He was sending his son to English and computer classes at a private school there, which cost fifty dollars a week. Then there was his broke and aging father, whose farm hadn't earned a profit in six years and who refused to take money from the *technicos* who asked him to lie about his acreage so they could steal half the subsidy themselves. And other, less urgent expenses: he couldn't resist buying American clothes for Nubia, knowing how fashionable they made her in Mexico, and he'd finally yielded to his son's tireless pleading and sent him a PlayStation 2 for Christmas. The rest of Ofelio's wages, what there were of them, went to rent and food and general necessities, whatever it took to get him from one day to the next.

He didn't blame his family about the gifts, of course: he'd felt the same way about American things before coming here, as if his life—his hopes and dreams and successes—were somehow inferior without them. He'd come here originally to pay off his debts so he wouldn't end up like his father, but also to relieve this sense of geographical misfortune.

Ofelio climbed the steps to his apartment, the smell of urine stinging his nostrils. His legs felt weak and waterlogged, as if he were trying to surface from the bottom of a lake. On his way to the fourth floor he passed the apartment below his, the doorway of which was knotted with people speaking clamorously in Chinese. The people were holding drinks and paper plates wilting with grease. He brushed through the crowd of guests, who lifted their plates to let him pass. Upstairs in his apartment, Ofelio's brother was lying in his boxer shorts on the foldout couch, watching an American talk show on TV.

"You're home early," he said in Spanish, surprised.

"I took the afternoon off."

"Loafer," his brother said, plumping the pillows behind his head. "You're lucky I'm not entertaining a woman friend." Adolfo worked the night shift as a janitor at a law office, which meant he slept much of the day until Ofelio came home. The different schedules made sharing a studio apartment bearable.

"They're having another party downstairs," Ofelio said, collapsing into a deep and mildewy chair in the corner. "That's the third one this week."

"Maybe it's a Chinese holiday." Adolfo put a finger on each temple and stretched the corners of his eyes, so that he looked like a squirrel.

"Last night she was singing in the middle of the night. The lady from downstairs. The tiny one? Singing at the top of her lungs." He'd have to discuss the singing with the lady's husband, a small, nervous-looking man with one ear shriveled into his head, like the coin slot in a vending machine. He saw the man all the time but had never spoken to him. Chinese people, with their fishy breath, made him sick to his stomach.

On TV, a woman with a microphone was interviewing policemen who'd posed for a sexy calendar. The policemen were wearing T-shirts that said OFFICER HUNK. When one of them stood up and took off his shirt, the audience of women hooted and pounded their feet. Ofelio asked his brother how he could watch such crap.

"It's very informative. I'm learning about law enforcement." Adolfo glanced at his own chest, which was flat and hairless. "Actually, I'm thinking about changing careers."

Ofelio managed a laugh. "You want to be a policeman?"

"There are many perks to this job." He gestured at the hooting women.

"I'd like to see you show up to police school without your papers." Ofelio suppressed a yawn, eyes blurring with tears. "Besides, if you were a cop, you'd have to deport me. I heard it on the radio: they just passed a law so that normal police can arrest us like *la migra*. They've already started in New York."

"You're a great pessimist, Ofelio. This is America. Everything's possible. You want me to be cleaning toilets the rest of my life?" Adolfo insisted he could be a policeman—it was just a matter of finding an American wife.

"My brother," Ofelio said gently. "You will never find an American wife with your hair like that. You look like a porn star."

He touched the back of his hair, which was shaved neatly on the sides but fell into a thick mane down his back. "What do *you* know? You're just a tourist, right? Like all the other *mojados*, visiting until they can return home to their countries."

Ofelio glanced back at the TV, ignoring his brother's sarcasm. He knew that everybody said they were returning to Mexico, if not immediately then in a year or two, and that most of them—except for the *braceros*, who spent their lives floating back and forth—never did. But

Ofelio was different. He didn't—like his brother, for example—try to live as an American on *mojado* wages. He never went out to eat and spent nearly every evening at home, except for two nights a week when he attended free classes at City College to sharpen his English. These past three years, working overtime until his feet bled, he hadn't even bought himself a new pair of boots. And the frugality had served him: he'd managed to pay off his debts, one week at a time. If he saved five thousand dollars, he could return home and have enough money to keep his son in school for the next year, perhaps even buy a piece of land near his father's. That was his dream: to start his own ranch. It wasn't so much, five thousand. The trick was, always, to remember his real life was elsewhere.

"Which reminds me," Adolfo said now, pointing at the picture of Nubia framed prominently on the window sill. "If your beautiful wife won't clean up after herself, I'm going to start charging her rent."

Ofelio blushed. In front of the picture was an open can of Coke and a single, untouched tamale resting on a plate. Every Sunday Ofelio would buy tamales from the Mexican grocery and sit beside his wife's photograph, pretending they were having dinner together—just as Nubia would set a place for him, extravagantly, at home. It was something they'd agreed to before he left. They'd never said it in so many words, but Ofelio knew it was a vow of some kind, a symbol of their not having dinner with anyone else.

A commercial came on TV for a store selling posturepedic mattresses. In the commercial, a crowd of insomniacs in pajamas were walking in a zombie-like mass through the streets and funneling into the entrance of the store, which glowed with a celestial light. The store was called Sleepland.

"Everything okay, brother?" Adolfo asked, eyeing him strangely.

"I need to lie down, I think."

Ofelio got up slowly and clunked across the room in his work boots and opened the door to the closet, which doubled as his sleeping quarters. He yanked on the twine hanging from the light bulb, and the light flickered on after a few seconds. He had to stand on the mattress in order to shut the door, balancing on the saggy edge where he'd sawed the mattress in half in order to fit it into the closet. Generally he slept on the foldout couch, unless Adolfo wasn't working and needed it himself. The arrangement had been fine at first, but for the past month they'd cut back Adolfo's hours at work, and Ofelio was sleeping in the closet three nights a week.

He sat on the mattress with his clothes on, keeping the light on for a minute in order to set his alarm clock. It was only 5:15, but he was planning to sleep through the night. As was his custom before bed, Ofelio reached into the corner of the closet and lifted the papier-mâché devil at his feet, weighing it carefully in his hands. His son had sent the two-foot doll with blue horns to him last fall, meaning for him to destroy it on *Santa Semana*, to blow it up with a firecracker as they did at home. Instead, Ofelio was using it as a piggy bank. He'd pierced a small hole between its legs where he could thread a hundred dollar bill rolled like a cigarette. It was something his brother would get a kick out of, that he was putting his earnings up the devil's ass. But it was his private savings, and he hadn't even told Adolfo about it.

Tonight, as always, the devil seemed to mock him, smirking at him from a bandido mustache and green polka-dotted face. Buey, it said, *you will never save enough money.*

Yes, I will. I've put two thousand in your ass already.

Ha! Try one thousand. That sounds more accurate.

I've been counting. You can't fool me, cabrón.

It's my ass. I should know what goes up it. Besides, do I feel any heavier?

Ofelio had to admit the devil did not feel heavier. He put it back in the corner and yanked off the light and lay stiffly in the dark. His muscles burned so much from heaving Sheetrock that he thought he might actually split into pieces, crack open like papier-mâché. Sometimes it was hard to separate the actual pain in his body with the pangs of longing he felt for his family. It was deeply physical, this longing. He missed them so much it felt like a second man trying to push from his torso, to struggle free of his bones. Thoughts of Nubia, in particular, made Ofelio's body hurt: the simple image of her neck, smooth as the girdled part of a tree when she lifted her hair, could keep him awake for hours. Touching himself helped, but often Ofelio's arms ached too much even to do that.

And then there were the other women, the ones he saw every day waiting for the train or talking to handsome men in restaurants or striding purposefully down the street with their eyes glued to the sidewalk. They were everywhere, stirring Ofelio's thoughts and clouding him with desire. At night, he'd imagine his wife above him and she would turn into someone else, a stranger he'd noticed on the street, some tall-booted woman who might slake his loneliness. Afterwards, cleaning himself with a T-shirt, he'd feel stained and miserable, scented with betrayal.

Adolfo's talk show had changed to something else, a toneless murmur jarred by a laugh track. Downstairs the festivities continued. Ofelio could hear Chinese laughter, pots clanking in the sink. He lay there for a long time, listening to the fugue of noises. In a little while, the city's lovers would steal off to their huge and beautiful beds, hugging each other to sleep if they were too wiped out to make love. Ofelio's throat felt parched. He realized, suddenly, that he couldn't bear another night in the closet. This was death, the dark constriction of a coffin. He opened the door and barged into the room, plucking his coat from the chair.

"I've got to get out of this apartment. Let's get a beer somewhere."

Adolfo regarded him in astonishment. "Who are you? Is this 1365 York Street? Where's Ofelio, my cheapskate brother who doesn't drink?"

"Still there," he said, gesturing at the closet. "Asleep."

Adolfo took him to a place on Bryant Street, a gringo bar he'd started frequenting in hopes of finding a wife. Ofelio looked around, taking note of the shiny new booths filled with young people dressed in disheveled, mismatched clothes. The walls of the bar were painted with stars and planets and flaming comets that seemed to be raining apocalyptically on the poorly dressed customers while they sipped their drinks. Ofelio was starting to have second thoughts about coming out, though he was glad he hadn't bothered to gel his hair. In the rear of the bar, behind the pool table, was a small stage with a single microphone centered in front of a stool.

"What is this '*neat-A*'?" Adolfo asked the bartender. He pointed at a banner over the stage that said OPEN MIKE NITE. Adolfo, though he'd been here for five years, spoke far less English than Ofelio.

"You mean 'night,'" the bartender said, laughing. "It's open mike tonight, which means anyone can perform. Fifteen minutes of fame."

Adolfo nodded, unwedging the slice of lime from his Corona. "These gringos can't spell their own language," he said in Spanish when the bartender had left.

The man sitting next to Adolfo started to tell a joke, entertaining two women who were standing at the bar with expressions of tolerant misgiving. The man was older than the other customers and had a short beard that he'd forked into two prongs with rubberbands. The joke was about an old lady who's magically granted three wishes. On her last wish, she asks that her poodle be transformed into an eighteen-year-old bodybuilder. "So that night she asks to see his pecker," the man said drunkenly, "but then the guy drops his pants and says"—he switched to a high-pitched voice—"'Bet you're sorry you had me neutered!'" When the two women failed to laugh, the man looked at Adolfo and Ofelio.

"What means 'pecker'?" Adolfo asked, smiling.

"You know," the man said, leaning toward him. "Cock. Schlong. I was being polite for the women." He looked at Ofelio helplessly and then pointed at Adolfo's crotch. "Peee-nuus," he said loudly.

Adolfo scowled. Someone called a name from the pool table in the back and the man got up, lurching from his stool. The two women said something to each other in private, glancing in the direction of the pool table before bursting into laughter. There was a spare stool next to Adolfo, and he stood up gallantly so the women could sit together. They declined the invitation, but he insisted, grinning in a way that concealed his silver tooth. Ofelio was embarrassed by his brother's chivalry; the feeling shamed him because he knew he wouldn't be embarrassed if the women were Latina.

The taller woman—a pale-skinned blond with freckles crowding her face—introduced herself, setting her glass on the bar in order to shake their hands. "Alden," she said, "like the pond, but without the 'W.'" She frowned, glancing from Adolfo to Ofelio and back again. She introduced her friend, whose face was puffed into an immobile grimace. The woman bowed her head, trying to smile through the paralysis of her lips. It was the first time Ofelio had ever seen a gringa blush in his presence.

"Gum surgery," Alden explained. "She didn't want to come out tonight, but I dragged her anyway."

The woman—Chloe was her name—hid her mouth with a napkin and tried to speak, but her voice sounded like a cassette tape after being warped by the sun. Ofelio couldn't make out a word she was saying. Alden urged her to show them what she really looked like, and Chloe rummaged through her purse and took out a photograph and passed it to Adolfo, who studied it for a minute before handing it to Ofelio. The picture showed an attractive woman in dark glasses standing next to a tremendous tree trunk.

"Sister?" Adolfo asked.

"Mnuhhhh," Chloe said. She pointed at herself, lifting a lock of her hair. Adolfo handed the picture back with a serious look, within which Ofelio guessed was the first minor cue of seduction.

"You too much more pretty than sister," he said.

The woman glanced at her friend in distress. Adolfo, perhaps relieved to be talking to someone whose English was worse than his, started to tell her about their own sister—a housekeeper in Salina Cruz—in half-mimed sentences. For his own part, Ofelio wasn't accustomed to drinking beer and found himself striking up a conversation with the freckled woman named Alden, who seemed impressed by his English. He told her about the classes he was taking at City College, how they spent an hour every Tuesday reading a book about successful immigrants.

"It's called *Sí, Se Puede,*" he said. "We talk about famous people. César Chavéz. Carlos Santana. We are supposed to be confident and follow our dream."

"Maybe I should take that class," she said, frowning. She told him that she was hoping to go to design school next fall but worked at a beauty store to pay the rent, selling expensive soap to tourists. She reached into her coat pocket and handed him a ball of soap, a brown sphere that looked suspiciously like a turd. He couldn't imagine anyone wanting to wash with it. "Keep it. Some distributor came by today and left a bunch of free samples."

Ofelio put the soap in the pocket of his own jacket. Alden studied his face for a second and then asked him where he was from, ducking her head forward to listen.

"Oh God," she said. "I love Oaxaca. I went there . . .what? Two years ago? The Night of the Radishes. And those little black animals—what do you call them?" She looked at him again and seemed suddenly embarrassed. "I suppose, being from Mexico, you probably wonder why we go berserk for this stuff. Crafts, I mean."

"Yes," he admitted. He supposed, in some way, it was related to his son's wanting a Playstation 2. "I don't really care about these things." He told her how the rug sellers in Oaxaca bought carpets from small towns near his father's ranch and then sold them for ten times the price. Very hard to make an honest living in the city. Before he could stop himself, he was telling her about his own failed business, the stranglehold of his debts, how he'd left Mexico when his wife was pregnant and had never even seen his two-year old daughter in person.

"Why doesn't your family come here?"

"It's very expensive. Also dangerous."

"That's terrible." Alden stared at her drink. "Oaxaca's so beautiful. You must think about it every day."

"Yes," he lied. In fact, he found himself thinking less and less of it, which alarmed him. The handsome buildings, the stray dogs in the *zócalo,* the sun like a weight on his face—he had to think now to remember them. It was one reason he was desperate to get home. And, of course, there were the things he felt guilty about not missing: the lines at the bank, say, or how when he bought flowers for Nubia, walking back to their house, machos used to taunt him from their cars and call him *mariposa.*

Alden asked him what it was he thought about most.

"My wife. Of course."

She smiled. "What's she like?"

"She is beautiful, but in a Mexican way. She loves food and is a bit *rechoncha.* I don't know how you say it in English? Plump? She's very smart too—when I had the business, she did all the accounts herself and saw over the customers. We are the perfect match." He glanced at Alden, ashamed at this idealized portrait of his marriage. "Of course, we argue too. Sometimes she is jealous. Before I leave for America, she became very upset. She sees the TV from the United States, you know, where every woman is thin. She yelled at me and says that I'll fall in love with a skinny American."

Alden closed her eyes for a few seconds, as if she were trying to memorize a phone number. Ofelio realized for the first time that she was drunk. He couldn't help noticing, despite the dim light of the bar, that even her eyelids had freckles on them.

"It must be very lonely without your family," she said, touching his arm.

Instinctively, Ofelio glanced over at his brother, surprised to discover that his stool was empty. He scanned the booths along the wall before spotting him near the pool table, waiting by the chalkboard and showing Chloe how to hold a cue. At that moment, a woman with a tattoo on her bicep and red streaks in her hair mounted the small stage at the rear of the bar. She sat on the stool and adjusted the microphone, lowering the pole so that it reached her mouth. The bar fell silent. She said she would read something she'd written, a poem called "Untitled: Prayer to Myself." *If only you would speak,* it began. The woman kept her head down while she read and refused to look at the audience, staring at her lap in a bout of shyness. Ofelio listened carefully but didn't understand what the poem meant, only that the woman kept repeating the word "savior." After a while, he realized that she wasn't bowing her head from shyness at all; rather, she seemed to be addressing her own sexual organ, beseeching it in a progressively louder voice:

"Deliver me from soap operas, from Doritos, from Walgreens in the afternoon.

You are the throb of a hummingbird's wings.

Wonderful savior! Pleasure! Float me to the sun."

The audience of customers clapped politely, waiting for the woman to climb off the stage. Americans seemed to be obsessed with genitalia. The depth of Ofelio's exhaustion, coupled with the two Coronas he'd drunk, was making him feel a bit unsteady, as if he were perched atop a ledge.

"I should bring my boss here to say a lecture," he said over the applause.

Alden looked at him oddly, cupping her ear as if she'd heard him incorrectly. He bought her another beer, and the bar grew quiet for the next reader, a man with a green patch under his lip like a slick of algae. Alden cocked her head while the man read into the microphone. The end of her hair skimmed Ofelio's arm, which was resting on the bar. Ofelio tried to focus on what was being said, hoping to learn some new words, but all he could think about was the feathery touch of her hair.

"My ex-boyfriend writes poetry," she said during the intermission. "Thierry, his name is. It's hard to pronounce, so I just call him 'asshole.' Sometimes he'll fast—not eat anything—for a whole week."

"Why?" Ofelio asked.

"To clear his thoughts. Like if he has an important decision to make."

"You mean like where to go to dinner?" he joked.

"No. God." She laughed. "It does seem kind of loco, doesn't it?"

Crossing the border, Ofelio had spent three days in a motel room with fourteen other people and no food. He'd felt like he might die. "Where is he now? This asshole?"

Alden looked down at her drink. "He dumped me. Three weeks ago. Fell in love with a woman from his yoga class. Hence the 'asshole.'" She lifted her glass in mock salute, a napkin clinging like a leaf to the bottom. "Actually, there are a lot of names. That's just the most versatile."

Ofelio reached over to remove the napkin from her glass and accidentally touched her sweater. He yanked his hand back just as their eyes met, a lingering glance. I should go home, he thought, standing up. Just then, a commotion broke out in the rear of the bar. He stood on his toes to get a better look and saw two men locked in an ardent struggle behind the pool table. The men were yelling, knocking into things as they fought. It took Ofelio a minute to recognize Adolfo. He was being overwhelmed by the man with the forked beard, shoved backward against the cue rack.

Drunkenly, Ofelio rushed through the lane of booths and bumped through a crowd of bystanders, grabbing the hulking man by the back of his shirt and trying to pull him off his brother. The man turned. Ofelio didn't see the punch so much as sense it, a psychic flash that sent him toppling to a seated sprawl against the jukebox. The world darkened and then returned, glittering in tiny specks. A rain of sequins. He'd never seen snow before, but imagined it would look as beautiful as this. He tried to focus his eyes, but only one of them seemed to work. The bass beat from the jukebox shuddered through his body. Eventually, someone helped him to his feet and steadied him against the wall before walking him toward the door. He couldn't follow what happened next except that they were sitting on the curb, he and Alden and Adolfo, the blindness in his eye opening to a bright and painful sliver.

Adolfo lit a cigarette and began smoking it in tiny puffs. His T-shirt was torn at the neck, hanging down like the flap of a tent. Otherwise, he seemed unscathed.

"What happened?" Ofelio asked. The world had stopped snowing, but his head felt damp and woolly.

"Fucking crazy gringo," Adolfo said in Spanish. "It was my turn to play pool. He said to stand back, because he was going to mop the floor with me. I understand 'mop'—but why the hell does he want to do it together? Crazy. I asked if he was the janitor of the bar, which is when he attacked me." He laughed and clapped Ofelio's shoulder. "Luckily, Ofelio Tyson stopped by to teach him a lesson."

"Where's Chloe?" Alden asked.

"*Se fue.* Mouth problem. No happy." He grinned at Ofelio. "I'd like to meet her sister," he said suggestively, slipping back into Spanish. He felt Ofelio's bicep with one hand and then raised his fists in a pugilistic stance. Crouched there behind his scrawny arms, he looked like a happy teenager. Adolfo checked his watch and bowed graciously at Alden, before running off to work with his hair bobbing behind him, punching the air with his fists.

It struck Ofelio, suddenly, that his brother was in despair—had been for many years. Alden leaned forward and examined Ofelio's eye, tipping his chin back to catch the light of the arc lamp. He could smell the sweat on her skin mingled with perfume. It was a damp earth smell, sweet and unpleasant at the same time.

"That's a real beauty. You better let me get some ice on it."

Ofelio stumbled back to his apartment, his head groggy from the stranger's punch. He had trouble opening the door, and Alden helped him fit the key into the lock. The place was a mess, dirty clothes thrown into a makeshift pile in the corner. He'd left the door to the closet open, and you could see the sawed-off mattress blocking the threshold. He wasn't embarrassed. It was his life. Not the one he would have chosen, but a life nonetheless.

Alden told him to lie on the foldout couch and then rummaged through the refrigerator and reappeared with something in her hand, a dish towel filled with foul-smelling ice. He would let her take care of him. He would allow this to happen—because his eye hurt and he was drunk and he liked the way she smelled—and then he would ask her to leave. Alden knelt beside him. He closed his eye and she nursed it with the towel, pressing gently until his face felt strange and conspicuous, a faint ache clutching his forehead.

"This should help the swelling," she said into his ear. Her voice was low and slurred. She glanced around the tiny studio, eyes sweeping the room before snagging on the window sill, studying the picture behind the Coke can and uneaten tamale.

"What's your wife's name?"

"Nubia."

"That's very pretty. Pretend I'm Nubia."

Something in Ofelio's heart chinked open, like a door. He closed his good eye as well, picturing his wife's face as she spoke to him. He liked that she had a gringa's voice, strange and untunable. He reached for her with his eyes closed. *Maybe we shouldn't,* the voice said, but he didn't listen, amazed at the boniness of her hips.

Ofelio woke to the sound of singing from downstairs. Chinese opera. He tried to sleep, but the singing continued, clawing through his ear and raking at his nerves. His eye throbbed in the dark. It went on for so long he thought he might actually cry. In a desperate fantasy, he imagined strangling the tiny woman with his bare hands, savoring the quiet as she slackened in his grip. Finally he got up and grabbed a broom from its place in the corner.

"*Cállate!*" He banged on the floor with the heel of the broom. The glass doors to the cupboards rattled in the kitchen. "Shut up!" he screamed in English. "You can't sing! Go back to China, you stupid-eye witch!"

The singing stopped. He turned, suddenly ashamed. Alden was sitting up in bed, her body white enough to locate in the dark. She mumbled something he didn't understand before lying back down and cocooning herself under the covers. Ofelio got back in bed and listened to the breathing next to him, the drunken rhythm so different from his wife's, too sick at heart to sleep.

The next day at work he roamed the eleventh floor in a daze, trundling wheelbarrows of debris and dumping them onto the platform of the freight elevator. Clouds of dust stung the raw skin at his eyebrow. Mr. Kitchens, framing his instructions like a concession to Ofelio's ineptitude, had decided it was a better idea to lift the debris out than to hurl it eleven stories to the dump truck. "Better stop looking in your neighbor's keyhole," he said, staring at Ofelio's eye. His coworkers were equally impressed by his appearance, regarding him with a new and curious respect. They threw air punches when he passed or veered out of his way in mock fright. Ofelio ignored them, too tired to respond. He could barely even lift the wheelbarrow without falling on his face. At one point he almost rolled himself right into the elevator shaft, not noticing that someone had ridden the platform down while he was away.

The crew stopped for a mid-morning break, smoking around the gangbox near the fire exit. Ofelio wiped the sweat from his eye; the morning had begun to heat up, fog lifting to reveal a smudge of sun. As he was folding up his jacket, the brown ball of soap Alden had given him fell out and rolled across the concrete.

"Jesus, Campos," one of the journeymen said, pretending to gawk. "They beat you up and shit in your pocket?"

Ofelio ignored the crew's laughter, too miserable to think of a comeback. He wondered if she was awake. He'd gotten up quietly, unable to face her in the light of dawn, and had left her in bed by herself. Well, his brother would be home by now—he could bid her farewell if she wasn't gone already.

He sat by himself near a stack of wallboard, touching the puffy curve of his eyelid to gauge its swelling. He had no idea how bad it was: since getting up, wretched from thoughts of Nubia, he couldn't bear to look at himself in a mirror.

After lunch, Ofelio swung by Mr. Kitchens's trailer to pick up his pay. He got there after the rest of the crew and was the last in line. Mr. Kitchens sat by himself with his hardhat upturned beside him, dispensing checks from a lockbox on his desk. A red crown circled his forehead from the band of the hardhat. The white workers ahead of Ofelio received their checks, signing their names into a filthy, grease-stained ledger before stepping aside to rip open their envelopes. The walls of the trailer were plastered with posters, bikini-clad women staring at Ofelio with slack-jawed mouths and slivered eyes, as if they'd been struck over the head with frying pans. Ordinarily the posters seemed like harmless wallpaper, but today they filled him with an obscure and welcome anger.

When he reached the front of the line, Mr. Kitchens counted out a stack of hundreds and handed them to him in a wad. Ofelio blinked, staring at the bills in his hand.

"*Me faltan dos cientos,*" he said, recounting them carefully. "You owe me two hundred."

Mr. Kitchens scribbled something in the ledger. "You're lucky I'm not a tightwad. It'll cost me more than that to replace the windshield. Not to mention the cab, which I'm banging out myself." He looked at Ofelio. "This is a business we're running—not a third-world orphanage."

Ofelio left the trailer and stopped about a yard or so from the entrance, squinting at a piece of rebar that was glinting in the dirt. The sun lay on his back without actually warming it. Beside the rebar, melting in a pool of colors, was a half-eaten popsicle of several different flavors. From the trailer he heard Mr. Kitchens talking about Wife's Pussy, extolling its freshness by comparing it to a mountain spring. *Swear to you, boys, you could bottle her fucking piss and sell it in Paris.*

It was the voice, lewd and declamatory at the same time, that drove him. Ofelio picked up the rebar at his feet and went back inside the trailer, the heat of the metal scalding his hand. He walked through the crowd of workers and grabbed Mr. Kitchens by the shirt and pulled him from his chair so that his sunburned face loomed close to his own, raising the rebar toward the ceiling like an axe. Mr. Kitchens gaped in astonishment. Ofelio stared into the shock of his boss's face, which seemed to have aged suddenly by thirty years, grown dumb and wide-eyed as a trout's. To his surprise, he noticed flecks of gray in his mustache. Except for Mr. Kitchens's panting, the room was silent. Ofelio closed his eyes for a second and pictured the face he was used to hating, imagining the nose shattering under his blow, the thin-lipped smile bashed into a blizzard of teeth. He could see everything perfectly. But when he opened his eyes again, all he saw was a scared and helpless man, lips trembling under a graying mustache, closer to the face he'd seen that day when Mrs. Kitchens scolded him on the street.

Ofelio let go of his boss, who slumped back into his chair like a puppet. He walked out of the trailer and across the sun-caked lot and all the way to the bus stop without looking back. The rage in his heart had disappeared, leaving only a deep and intimate weariness. On the bus, the driver studied him warily before closing the doors, observing him in the giant mirror above his head, as if Ofelio were a drunk out to make trouble. His eye twitched in a painful rhythm unconnected to his pulse. It wasn't until Ofelio had settled into a window seat near the back that he realized he was still holding the rebar. Watching the world pass by his window—the commuters speeding past the bus with cell phones cuddled to their ears, wearing suits or glasses or uniforms—the reality of what he'd done sank in. He'd lose his job. There was no way around it. He had seven hundred dollars in his pocket, all of which he'd have to wire to Oaxaca. There was next month's mortgage to pay off, his son's tuition. Even if he found a new job in a week, he'd lose six days' wages. The thought of spending any of the money in his closet—what he was saving for his ranch—made him utterly depressed.

He had a vision, a terrible fantasy, of the papier-mâché devil broken on the bed, Alden ducking down the street to buy herself some expensive clothes.

When he got home, Ofelio rushed upstairs and flung open the closet. The devil was still there, leering and bandido-faced. Ofelio knelt there on the mattress while a hubbub of voices jabbered below him. Incredibly, his downstairs neighbors seemed to be having another party. He stalked down the steps in an angry fog. A Chinese couple who looked to be about Ofelio's age were standing in the threshold, drinking from teacups. Through the open door, he could see some kids running around inside the apartment, chasing each other and shrieking like monkeys.

"What's happening here?" Ofelio asked the people in the doorway. "It's two-thirty in the afternoon!"

"My father-in-law," the man said gravely, in unaccented English. He held the porcelain teacup with two hands, which were veinless and perfectly manicured. They were the most beautiful hands Ofelio had ever seen. "He passed away on Tuesday. Mr. Tan. Very sudden." He tilted his head, squinting at Ofelio. "Did you know him?"

"No," Ofelio said, taken aback. *"Poquito.* Only by eye. I live upstairs."

The man studied him carefully. He raised one of his beautiful hands and gripped Ofelio's arm at the shoulder.

"I can see it's a shock," he said. "Come in and have some tea with us."

Despite Ofelio's protests, the man kept his hand where it was and piloted him into the room, an immaculate studio with a layout identical to his brother's. For a minute, in his trance-like exhaustion, Ofelio had the disconcerting impression that he'd wandered into his own apartment. There were flowers arranged in plastic vases, a calendar on the wall with a picture of a puppy on it. Ofelio walked in slowly, wary of disturbing the gathering. He saw now that it wasn't actually a party, but a handful of relatives assembled in mourning. Mrs. Tan was sitting by herself at a plastic table in the kitchen area, eyes raw from weeping. She dabbed at her face with a kitchen sponge. She was so small that her feet barely reached the floor. Ofelio's boots squeaked, and the tiny woman looked at him, her face bright with tears. He realized he'd been mistaken those times in the middle of the night, that she must have been wailing in grief.

Ofelio bowed his head, a flush of shame heating his face. It seemed remarkable that an entire life could be lived here, that someone could grow old and die in a space no bigger than this. The man with beautiful hands steered him around the couch, avoiding the children scampering through the room. On the window sill, arranged like an altar, was a framed picture of Mr. Tan. The picture had been taken from a clever angle, so you couldn't see the shriveled slot of the man's ear. Ofelio felt something—a coldness—slink across his scalp. Crowding the picture, among other offerings, was an open can of Coke and a plate laden with gluey white buns.

He let the man with beautiful hands lead him past the window and ease him into a chair.

The next week Ofelio tried to find a job, hunting around at construction sites he'd heard about from his former coworkers, taking buses all the way to Alameda or San Leandro or Mill Valley before discovering they didn't need him. The economy was bust: why hire *illegales* when they could get Americans for the same rate? Eventually he gave up looking for construction work and tried to get a job like his brother's, cleaning toilets or washing dishes. He combed the newspaper for openings, impatiently, but couldn't find a thing.

After a few weeks he took the papier-mâché devil from his closet and smashed it open on the floor of his apartment. Two thousand bucks, as he'd thought. Seeing the shattered doll like that, headless and forlorn, gave him a grim sort of pleasure. He stuck half the money under his mattress for reserve. After allotting five hundred for his family, he went to a store on Mission Street and bought himself a new pair of boots, walking the aisles to make sure they were comfortable. The sales clerk steered him toward a shirt, a plaid one with a handsome cut. Ofelio liked the colors. Paying for the clothes at the cashier counter, he felt an odd lifting in his heart, as if someone had forgiven him a debt.

Adolfo came home the next morning and saw the shards of devil still scattered on the floor. He foraged a blue horn from the corner. Ever since discovering Alden in his bed, he'd looked at Ofelio differently, like a boy who'd seen through a magician's trick. "I work all night cleaning floors, and what happens?"

"I'll pick it up," Ofelio said. "Get off my back."

Adolfo turned away, disgusted. "I don't mind sweeping out your women, but you'll have to clean up after your fights."

That night Ofelio called his family, who were waiting by the phone. His daughter was learning the noises for animals and made a sound like a sheep. Ofelio did his best to laugh. He tried talking to his wife, but the careless affection in her voice made him queasy and he had to get off.

Of course, he hadn't told his family about attacking Mr. Kitchens and losing his job, or that he'd started going down to Cesar Chavez

Street every morning, waiting for work with the other day laborers. The laborers had made him take a vow, ensuring he wouldn't work for less than ten dollars an hour. It didn't seem to make much sense, given the number of people lining the sidewalk. On the rare occasion when a car pulled up, they raced each other to the curb and smothered it from all sides, whistling through their teeth. More often than not, no one picked Ofelio up and he'd stand there all morning with the sun baking his face, staring at the bank of fog receding from the hills of Twin Peaks.

Some of the laborers had only been in the city a week or so, arriving there from places like Conchagua or Zacatecas or Guatamala City. Ofelio found himself helping the new arrivees with their English. He taught them words, sounding each one carefully while they watched his lips. *Sky. Shoelace. Apart.*

One morning, sitting against the wall of a karate studio, he saw Alden and her friend crossing the street on their way from Precita Park. They were laughing about something, their heads tipped back at the same angle. Ofelio hid his face and didn't wave.

Later, a red pick-up slowed in front of him and stopped a little way down the curb, but he let the other laborers run after it and didn't get up. It felt too nice to sit. Rent was due in a few days, but he still had plenty of money—he'd stopped counting it, since delving into the bills under his mattress. He used to sit like this as a boy sometimes, leaning against the wall of their ranch house when he was supposed to be shucking corn for dinner, making Adolfo do all the work while he drifted off to sleep. The men shouted at him from the bed of the pickup. He was half asleep already, lost to the drowsy orbit of his thoughts. He remembered that day in the Chinese woman's apartment—how exhausted he'd been, as if his head was packed in clay, and how the man with beautiful hands had guided him to a chair, mistaking him for a mourner. He could feel the hand now, pressing his shoulder. "Make yourself at home," the man had said, and Ofelio had all but forgotten who he was, such a relief it seemed to rest.

Eric Puchner is a Wallace Stegner Fellow at Stanford University. His short stories have appeared or are forthcoming in *Zoetrope: All Story, Glimmer Train, Cimarron Review* and *Quarterly West* as well as the *Pushcart Prize* and *Best New American Voices* anthologies. He was the recipient of a 2002 Joseph Henry Jackson Award for young California writers. He lives in San Francisco, where he is completing a collection of stories.

INTERCESSION TO SAINT BRIGID/
Anthony Butts

Young and black, a woman rocks back and forth
on the Greyhound to Dallas, a fulcrum of night
in her white T-shirt. A white woman farther back

dressed in black scratches the top of her head with one
fingernail like a record skipping over some song
she'd love to remember, some ode she seems

to never give up on. White crosses grow larger
in their trinities the farther we descend toward
the equator, Southern culture like those high-

powered lights turned at dizzying angles upward,
faith illuminated in an attempt at the largest
manuscripts ever read. Saint Brigid is back

on Lake Michigan, The Book of Kells in my lap,
the lamp light above my head faintly culling
stronger strands from weaker ones as no one

pays attention to me or my red jersey
in the obscurity of that near-coffin rolling,
its tubular presence like the shape of a life—

that form the only person at a party who's
interesting. I will not let go of that raft.
Islands of light. Eyes of night. Fist-sized

towns pass incredulously by. Sometimes a person
pointing aimlessly on the corner is like a pattern
interwoven in daylight, a labyrinth of sound and sight,

runes of our fate known to someone save ourselves:
the Lady of the Lake, her hair as dark as the two
women on board. One has scratched a small

hole in her head, blood collecting in the tiny "u"
in her psyche. The other sits with her small girl
mewling to a music only her mother could know.

And I am all fretwork, or so I believe, in this moment
where the next buses will connect with the terra-cotta
mountains of Utah and the windswept plains of Nebraska—

upon the blackout of intercessions as darkness closes
ranks at 1:16 A.M., about an hour before Dallas where
we'll wake into the only light we'll witness on this night.

MIST AND FOG/*Anthony Butts*

Saucers and their cousins sit respectfully in silence,
the room austere in black-and-white distressed checks
lining the Formica like footprints to nowhere, two rooms
separated by more than just dusky effervescence, Saint Brigid

come ashore in the form of mist and fog. Outside, there is no
word for *demure* or *dapper* as gray inhabits both places
of the mind—the last rays persevering beneath sky's
observation, the Lady of the Lake seeing a whistle's billowing

with her ears. We rely upon odd senses when in need,
the couple muttering each one to themselves as if
those cluttered rooms were populated by thoughts,
as if throw pillows were like faces passing in the reflection

of department store windows—each shopping
for their own anniversary gift, which no one thought
to give. Squirrels gather the world into their own
constituency of promise and fortitude as if no other

were available, contemplative winter a sustaining
memory of more than luck and loss. Vibration
of missing sound after rhythmic chanting is like
the course of human history turned around:

a congregation in the loss of languages spoken
and unspoken after group meditation, after the hum
of Saint Brigid has inspired even the leaves to sing
along. Sound can only hurt you if you let it,

the couple somnambulistic in the kitchen
organizing saucers according to their own
phenomenology, the eerie mist above
the dishes like miniature gymnasts

twisting in the rhythm of sentences turning:
words bending thoughts like light refracted—
the couple making love with their gestures,
even if mist is not yet in their eyes.

SONG OF EARTH AND SKY / *Anthony Butts*

The sun rises in its happenstance of the day,
garbage trucks like predawn crickets, the lack
of streetwalkers as its own object of desire,

life more like art than the reality we reconstruct
through daily ritual imitated. Routine is candy
for the psyche, blocks of caramel on a park bench

like children sitting calmly, a jar of chocolates
individually wrapped on His table at home
in the only version of heaven I must know.

Uncle Vanya on stage, young actors allowing
their own characters to slip through at unwarranted
intervals, the black and white of the play like

a photograph developing in liquid depths
of hydroquinone the dark room indistinguishable
from the substance, Doctor Astrov imperceptible

to his own logic. This is what makes them great,
that reservoir of happenstance called upon in
ruff-hewn hours of practice and malcontent

like great swatches of heaven in the form of
inspiration when blue is the only color
assigned to the soul of an artist looking

skyward, when platinum orange is the color
of subsistence before the morning star
as the great Sky God leans in for

a peek at the day and what we might bring.
He is as hokey as all that because no other
emotion is as pure, is as metallic as ice

in the way that it looks to others, that sentiment
seeming more like the pocket miracle of
a plastic lighter, transparent and purple

before the tip of the cigarette which might
not serve as inspiration but more like a
partner with whom the would-be Astrov

might dialogue as if its white dress were
would-be wedding attire, as if Sonya would
wait forever for her man to come around.

Sky knows more than earth will tell it,
our own fates here just as easily unwrapped
and tasted like the most forbidden of sweets,

the choicest of produce in the marketplace of our
longing because perseverance from "here" to "there"
is like the last sentimental cricket inching home.

Anthony Butts is a member of the creative writing faculty at Carnegie Mellon University
in Pittsburgh and the author of *Fifth Season* (1997) and *Little Low Heaven* (2003). His work
has appeared in numerous journals and anthologies.

A GOOD BOY/*Cynthia Morrison Phoel*

FOR HOURS NOW Dobrin has been begging Stassi to stop it, shut up, are you *trying* to make her mad? "Put those down," he hisses, whispering, though his mother lags too far behind to hear.

Stassi has plucked two tomatoes from his bag and is holding them to his chest, the stems pointing out. "Dobrin*e*," he says, cupping the undersides of the tomatoes with mock tenderness. "You want a squeeze?"

"*Molya ti si*," Dobrin pleads. He has had enough of his friend. They have spent the entire afternoon together, helping his mother in the garden she keeps a half-hour's walk up the mountain. Until today Dobrin had almost liked the garden, mostly for the gratification it brought his mother, who hardly had time for it. Now Stassi has tainted the place, not to mention the tomatoes, which no amount of washing will ever make clean. "Your mother's tomatoes are so *firm*," Stassi said the first time she turned her back. "So deliciously *ripe*." By the time they were finished in the garden, Stassi was saying things right in front of her, as if his comments were so clever she would never catch on.

He finally shut up when they began the walk home, but at the crest of the hill overlooking their town, Dobrin's mother stopped to talk to an old woman. It irritated Dobrin that there could be so many old women and that his mother could not pass a single one of them without stopping to say hello. He continued down the road with Stassi, which turned out to be a mistake. Away from Dobrin's mother, Stassi started up again.

"Some nipples really are green, you know," he says now, admiring his handheld protrusions.

Dobrin can see his mother inching away from the woman, trying to extricate herself from the conversation she started. It is still early, and already they are on the brink of evening, the sun low over the mountain.

Dobrin is ready for the summer to be over. Stassi will be in his class again, but there will be others there to dilute his energy and Mrs. Kuneva there to squelch it. Many of his classmates think it unfair that they should be stuck with crabby old Kuneva for a second year in a row, but Dobrin doesn't mind so much—certainly not so much as he minds Stassi fondling the tomatoes.

"If you don't stop it—" he begins but is distracted by a tomato bouncing down the mountain. He squats to trap it, and another hurtles by, another and another. A throng of tomatoes has escaped from one of the bags. Above him, his mother stands in the middle of the street, shading her eyes. Her bag of tomatoes, what's left of it, is tipped at her feet.

A quickening in Dobrin's stomach and he follows her gaze, panning church steeple and bakery stack, flagpole displaying limp Bulgarian flag, rusted metallic beams of the new post office, started but never finished, the skyline of flat asphalt roofs. Finally, with Stassi beside him pointing, Dobrin sees it. In the hours they have been at the garden, the large white moon of a satellite dish has appeared on top of an apartment building. Theirs.

"*Bozhe*," Stassi says, "Do you think your father—"

"I think you should go home," Maika says. She is walking fast now, about to overtake them.

Stassi nods politely to Dobrin's mother, and then, looking at Dobrin, his face splits with a grin too wide to be merely a smile. He makes a great show of running down the mountain unencumbered, flailing his arms out from his sides, going out of his way to stomp on tomatoes lolling in the road.

Dobrin's mother continues down the road, neither waiting for Dobrin to retrieve Stassi's bag nor slowing for him to catch up. By the time he is balanced with a bag in each hand, his mother is several paces ahead. Something advises him to keep his distance.

After a block or so of trailing Maika, of silence and double-the-bags bumping, leaking smeary tomato juice down his legs, the satellite dish disappearing from his vision but growing larger in his mind, he wishes Stassi were still there.

Dobrin's father greets them at the apartment door with jumpy hellos. In the next room a cheery, televised voice offers a more articulate welcome. "Your ticket to the best in sports," it promises. "World Cup soccer. Watch it here."

"You," Maika says and rushes past him.

Dobrin's father flinches, though only for a moment. He has been expecting this. This is not the first time he's accepted *electronica* instead of wages, though this piece, this infraction, is the biggest by far.

In the days that follow, Dobrin can hardly last an hour without going outside to admire the dish. Up close it's dizzyingly large, and Dobrin is at once thrilled and sickened by how big it is. Even from a distance it is otherworldly and menacing.

Stassi says that with a dish like this Dobrin can have any girl he wants. He says girls can't resist a really big dish. This dish is going to change Dobrin's life. Dobrin wonders if it already has, though not in the way

Stassi thinks. Of course there have been fights before, too often having to do with the cost of Dobrin's notebooks or the condition of his shoes or the new jeans, too tight too soon. Though small for his age, Dobrin would be willing to stop growing if it would make things between Maika and Tatko a little easier.

But Dobrin cannot think of one fight where the crime was committed with intent. He does not like trouble, least of all with his mother, who has skinny shoulders and is not at all pretty when she's angry. Tatko, on the other hand, does not seem to mind trouble—a thing Dobrin can't quite grasp. Sometimes he wishes his father would be nicer to Maika or at least not make her so mad. Other times, he thinks it takes a lot of guts. It takes a lot of guts to own a dish this big. He wonders if guts grow along with belly, muscle and bone.

Sitting on his mountain perch, Dobrin stares absently at the dish, which looms over their home like a big white cloud. Beneath its shiny orb the rest of the building looks shabby and old. Better when he makes his eyes into slits and looks only at the dish. Then, what he sees is glory.

How long can Dobrin's parents go without speaking to each other? A week has passed, and so far nothing more than the occasional spray of words spat out like watermelon seeds—necessary, unwanted. Dobrin is on the lookout for a sign—a *Bless you* or *Excuse me*, a stifled giggle— any indication that they will be okay.

Stassi assures him the silence is normal. Parents can go for long periods of time without talking. He asks if Dobrin can hear sex noises coming from their bedroom because if they're having sex, then they're going to be okay. "Sex can cure anything," Stassi says. "Even cancer."

What does Stassi know? His parents have been divorced since he was four. He has never known anyone with cancer *or* a satellite TV.

Dobrin thinks that if Maika would just sit down and watch one of the TV's programs, she might learn to appreciate it. But she refuses to enjoy it. It's foolish to own a satellite TV, she says, when you can barely afford heat. This year she is teaching Bulgarian literature at both high schools in town. At night and on weekends she tutors private students at the dining room table. During these hours the TV should not be on, though there have been more than a few crucial matches—Barcelona, mostly, and sometimes Munich—that Tatko has watched with the volume muted.

Dobrin has to agree with Tatko that the satellite TV is a blessed thing. Even with his parents not talking he loves it. After years of watching the same three stations through a thick haze of electric fuzz, it seems like a miracle that there can be so many programs playing at once and no matter where the program is coming from, the picture is clear—clearer than the hand in front of your face. Clearer even than the mural pasted to their living room wall of a sun setting on a crystalline lake, an image that always looked remarkably sharp until now. Soccer and basketball all day long, and if there isn't a new game on, they replay an old one. At night, after Maika goes to bed, girls appear on the screen—girls like Dobrin has never imagined, like the centerfolds on the front of the bus only better, touching themselves, undulating with passion. It is better than his cousin's Madonna video, better than anything he has ever seen.

During the matches Dobrin cheers and Tatko jumps up and down, calling fouls and assigning penalty shots like a true referee. But the girls they watch in silence. Tatko—and Stassi, when he's there—on the sofa, Dobrin in an overstuffed chair. Dobrin's favorite is a girl called Lana, schoolteacher by day, hooker by night. At school Lana wears heavy glasses, long skirts and blouses buttoned up to the neck. Dobrin thinks that if he were her student, he would only consider her a little bit beautiful. Then, the camera does this great thing where it peers between the buttons of her blouse and transports you to the other Lana, the unconscionably gorgeous Lana with parts Dobrin can hardly believe are real.

They watch the girls with the volume turned low because Maika is sleeping in the other room. Tatko insists there are parts of a man's education a mother shouldn't know about, and for the wondrous hours with Lana and others, Dobrin is willing to agree. Besides, he suspects the girls might make Maika's migraines worse than they already are. As it is, on most nights she goes to bed without even having dinner. Sometimes, through the closed door, Dobrin can hear his mother's gasps as the pain grips and squeezes her brain. If he goes in to check on her, he finds tears soaking her pillow. Tatko says the headaches are an act to make him feel bad. Dobrin is not so sure; nevertheless, he can feel his father's sadness, the way he slumps over the arm of the couch and peers at the TV from beneath the low visor of his hand. Even when they are watching girls, he can feel it.

It's almost impossible to believe that the girls on TV and Mrs. Kuneva are of the same species. Stassi says people shrivel up if they don't have sex. Dobrin points out that neither he nor Stassi is having sex, and neither is as withered and sorry as Kuneva.

"Who says I'm not having sex?"

"*Stiga be.* Who would have sex with you?"

"Your mother," Stassi screams and slaps his leg. "You thought you had her all to yourself, didn't you?"

Dobrin punches Stassi in the arm, says, "Stop with my mother!" and Stassi laughs harder. This is the Stassi Dobrin hates. In seventh grade he was responsible for the extra homework their class got almost every night, homework that Stassi himself never did. He was always rocking his chair, tipping his desk, dropping bits of chalk into Mrs. Kuneva's cups of espresso, spoiling what little stamina she had to get through class. As they embark on eighth grade, Dobrin expects more of the same. To Dobrin, sameness is more ominous than change.

On the first day of school, Mrs. Kuneva addresses them as *ladies and gentlemen*. "Ladies and gentlemen, take out your English workbooks," she says with such propriety that for a moment Dobrin thinks she may have forgotten where she is. He looks at his classmates—Stassi with his head bent over the desk, using a protractor to engrave his name in the already mutilated surface—and wonders if it's possible that they have become *ladies and gentlemen*. Indeed, they have grown. Taller, wider, moister. They have more hair. But *ladies and gentlemen?* From Stassi's corner of the classroom comes a fit of coughing and inaudible words.

In their second year with Kuneva, Dobrin's classmates know to be skeptical of their teacher's broad optimism. Last year she was always making them out to be more than what they were. "You are very well prepared for this exam," she would say as they embarked on a test that half of them would fail. "You know all the words in this dictation," she'd promise before she read an impossible passage. "You are the most considerate group of students I have ever had," she told them a week before Women's Day, and still they gave her only a paltry bouquet, picked from a garden near the school and wrapped in paper towels. Time and again they witnessed the rise and fall of her hopes. And still, Dobrin believed that maybe he would do well on this exam, this dictation.

That first day of school, Mrs. Kuneva seems to be hoping for an awful lot. She is all dressed up like a lady out of one of those films from the British Council that she is always making them watch. She wears a pink dress, cinched at the waist. It might look nice if her breasts weren't so saggy and thin. Her hair is curled, pinned just above the ears. She looks like an antique—girlish and nicotine yellow—and you can tell she fancies herself a beauty, the way she walks around kicking her pink shoes out in front of her. Dobrin wishes she looked prettier than she does. It's a shame because he can tell how hard she's tried.

Later Dobrin catches Kuneva grimacing at her saggy self in the smudged classroom window. Already she has confiscated the protractor and a soccer ball from Stassi and worked herself into a healthy rage over their poor memories. She has dictated a passage that she pledged would be "so simple they would enjoy it." Sharpening his pencil, Dobrin momentarily believed in his proficiency in the English language—he would start this school year off with a high mark!—only to stumble first on *Somerset*, then on *Maugham*. By the second sentence, he knew he would be lucky to get a passing mark.

Ladies and gentlemen, Kuneva says as she bids them good-bye. When he tells his mother about this, she catches her breath—*Gospodin? Kak mozhe?*—then starts to cry. She says she is not ready for him to be a man just yet.

After school, Stassi invites himself over to watch the satellite TV. Soon this becomes a habit. "Only if you leave before my mom gets home," Dobrin says, feigning irritation. The truth is, he is glad for an ally when he returns to the apartment at the end of the day.

In just a few weeks the TV has attracted a number of Tatko's friends, four or five of them, who come in the morning and stay all day. By the time Dobrin gets home from school, they have nothing left to say to each other. They just sit there, flaking peanut skins into their chest hair and watching. Distracted by the scratching and belching and crunching on nuts, Dobrin can hardly follow the program on the screen. At least Stassi talks, he finds himself thinking. At least he can count on Stassi to break a silence.

Today Stassi leans over and whispers, "Your dad's got boobs," eyeing Tatko, shirtless.

Dobrin tweaks Stassi's forearm until he says *ow*, but Stassi's right; Tatko does have boobs. Dobrin worries that he will grow boobs too. He hopes that this won't happen until he's married, or at least until he's twenty or eighteen.

In the meantime, he wishes his dad would stop walking around bare-chested all the time. At the pool, Tatko's boss makes him wear a shirt, though he doesn't mind if Tatko rolls up the sleeves to get an even tan across his biceps. Dobrin thinks he looks impressively strong when he does this. Tatko's arms are broad and flat and three times the circumference of Dobrin's.

Some of the other men are wearing shirts, but not all. Nudging Stassi, Dobrin nods at one of the men with boobs as big as Tatko's. Immediately he is sorry to have drawn this comparison. They are not the same, his father and these men. *His* father has a job. *His* father has a satellite TV.

A barman at the pool café, Tatko works from May until September. Only from September to May does he sit on the couch, and even then, not all the time. Once or twice a year he manages to pick up a week here or there, waiting tables at a conference or tending to a private party. When that happens, there's a feast at home, with meat and yellow cheese and a bottle of perfume for Maika, presented with great flourish in front of friends, the price tag still on.

Back when they were talking, Maika used to plead with Tatko to find another job. She would come home with ideas for him. "Marietta says Nikolai has more work than he can handle." Or, "Stefan says they're looking for a repairman at the motel." But Tatko would get angry and say he made parties, not repairs. He was waiting on the couch for something good to come his way.

These days Dobrin would relish such an argument. He suspects it is not Tatko's joblessness that perpetuates Maika's anger so much as it is the couch sitting and the satellite TV. Even Maika knows there are not enough jobs to go around this town. It's likely Tatko couldn't get another one even if he tried.

To make up for the rest of the year, when summer comes around, Tatko works long hours. From dawn until dusk he serves *kebabche* and beer and keeps the shrill *chalga* music turned up high. He stands behind the grill and calls to his cluster of tables—a slab of cheese? some bread? a little Ruska salad?—spreading around a spirit of plenty. His customers buy it, ordering food and drink as they rarely do at restaurants, as though this is some great celebration. Every few minutes, Tatko raises his hands and snaps his fingers and rotates his hips. "Oh, ho," he calls, caught up in the swirl of his own good humor. Chef, waiter, bartender, no one takes better care of customers than he.

Tatko's bar is the only profitable part of a business that should do better than it does. The next pool being three villages away, there is little competition. This pool is clean and well kept and chlorinated enough to kill all the germs. What's more, nestled at the foot of the mountain, it gives the effect of swimming in a big green cavern. But Vulkov, Tatko's boss, keeps the prices high. People have to ration their trips to the pool, saving their *leva* for the most beautiful days. They come more frequently at the end of the summer, once they have given up hope of affording a trip to the Black Sea. But it is not enough to make up for the earlier months. When Vulkov pays Tatko at the end of the summer, his fifteen-hour days, his boundless energy, they do not matter. Vulkov says he can offer more if Tatko will accept electronics—*TV, stereo, VCR, you pick*—in lieu of cash. Tatko is pleased to make the deal.

Hearing Maika's key in the door, Dobrin wonders if Tatko is still pleased with the deal he made. A week ago he told the couch-sitters,

"Next year, CD player," but he hasn't mentioned it again. As Maika passes through the room she deliberately steps in front of the TV. "Extravagances," she hisses, grabbing glasses and bowls off the table and out of hands. "Look at this mess." Dobrin wishes she wouldn't do this—it embarrasses everybody—but this, he suspects, is her aim.

The men leave, but not before Tatko retorts, "You have your extravagances, I have mine." He is talking partly about the Cadbury eggs that Maika buys for Dobrin and the food she puts out on their first-floor balcony for stray dogs and cats. But mostly he is talking about the money Maika spends on migraine remedies. Once a month she goes to see a woman for treatments. Vilichka claims to have extra-sensory powers, which she uses to put spells on water and herbs and animal fats that people buy to cure migraines and burns and other afflictions. She claims she can cure anything, and she has a great many followers who believe in her. Maika pays ten *leva* for the bus ride, thirty *leva* for the visit, and one hundred *leva* for ten gallons of water, which Dobrin has to help her carry back on the bus.

"If you're going to spend that kind of money, at least go to a doctor," Tatko says. It's not so much money, really, but it's been a long time since there's been store-bought wine on the table or a stick of dried meat to eat. Dobrin knows that if Tatko ever saw Vilichka, there would be no end to his fury. For as much as Dobrin wants to believe that Vilichka can help his mother, instinct tells him that she's a fake. It's not that Vilichka doesn't look the part; it's that she looks *too* much like the earthy, spiritual vessel of energy she claims to be. She wears long skirts and grows her hair down to her bottom. She doesn't even wear a bra, which Dobrin finds terribly distracting when she's bending over the spigot in her yard, helping them fill the jugs. Her breasts are the largest he's ever seen, too big, if that's possible. He thinks if she were really serious about her work, she would at least wear a bra and roll her hair into a bun.

Once Tatko claimed he had poured Vilichka's water out of the jug and replaced it with regular water and Maika didn't even notice. Maika cried when he said this.

Tonight, Maika endures her headache long enough to eat dinner. Afterward, she cooks rice in the fat leftover from their meal, and Dobrin helps her carry it out to the balcony. Hearing the scrape of the metal bowls on the cement floor, the dogs and cats come running from all around, rib cages heaving, whimpering happiness. They lick Maika's hands, they are so grateful. When a dappled bitch with a freshly torn ear nuzzles its nose between Dobrin's legs, an embarrassing knot rises in his throat. He wonders about the difference, if one exists, between extravagance and need. Vilichka's remedies, the way Maika suffers, isn't the cost trifling for the possibility of relieving her pain? Even the satellite TV doesn't seem like much of an extravagance when you consider how much use it gets. "Business," Tatko's friends call it, because this is what they have to do all day, and the fact of the big white satellite dish atop the building—doesn't that count for something?

Later on, Dobrin asks Tatko why the men never leave until it's too late. Apparently this is funny. "You think it's better at their homes than at ours?"

A month of warp and confusion, a kaleidoscope of worries shifting in a round. At night Dobrin lies in bed and listens for sex noises, laughter, the opening and closing of the bathroom door. Granted these sounds have been missing before and they always, eventually, came back. Nevertheless he has noticed that the spaces between them have grown longer and quieter, and he wonders about the time when they stop connecting altogether and all they have left is the consoling chatter of the satellite TV.

Dobrin thinks that if Tatko would apologize, Maika might accept what has already been done. It would make a difference if she knew that he was sorry. But Tatko's jaw is set; his arms are crossed; his eyes are fixed on the TV. Who is he to apologize when he is not even sorry? How can he be sorry for this glorious TV?

Barking erupts outside Dobrin's window. The belated heat makes the dogs surly and tired. Mrs. Kuneva says Americans call this Indian summer, this last burst of warm weather before it turns cold. To Dobrin it feels like a taunt—an aftertaste of the summer just past and a reminder that the next summer is a long way off.

By his measure, it had been a good summer, perhaps even a great one. As in summers past, he spent most of his days at the pool, where Vulkov let him swim and eat for free. Staying home was not a good idea. When he stayed home, Maika got cross. She said she wanted to get *something* out of this arrangement. They couldn't eat a stereo, she would start in. Dobrin couldn't wear a VCR to school.

At the pool, Vulkov had Dobrin fill in when the lifeguard didn't show up. This made Dobrin nervous—he had not been trained to rescue people—but Vulkov said it didn't matter. People would feel safer and behave better with someone in the chair. Once his initial unease passed, Dobrin looked forward to the times Vulkov pushed his fat finger into Dobrin's bicep and pointed toward the seat. He was something of a celebrity on these days. Everyone wanted to talk to him and hang out by his chair. He suspected that they were mainly interested in talking to a lifeguard and not so much to him. Nevertheless, he could not help but be enamored with how brown his feet looked against the light blue platform of the chair and with the girls' decorated toenails and pastel-colored bikinis that turned almost see-through when they got wet.

On top of the sheets, wearing only his underwear, Dobrin can almost believe that summer is still here. That just hours ago he was sitting in the lifeguard chair, staring down at the girls from his class, pondering the twin miracles of their breasts. Just as Dobrin slips his hand beneath the elastic band of his underpants, a man starts yelling at the dogs to shut up. A woman screams at the man. A chorus erupts on the street outside. Dobrin wants to yell too—aren't they supposed to be smarter than dogs?—but instead of adding to the noise, he gets up, leans out the window, and spits out the big glob of phlegm that has gathered in his throat.

"Dobrin? Dobrin Kirilov, was that you?" an angry voice yells from below.

A month ago, Dobrin would have apologized for spitting on his downstairs neighbor. Now, he lies back down and wraps a pillow around his ears.

"Ladies and gentlemen, take out your English workbooks." By the end of October, Dobrin's class has proven that they are nothing of the sort. Still, Kuneva starts out every morning the same way, with hope and expectation that they will have done their homework and come prepared to participate in class.

Likewise, Dobrin, at the end of October, still starts out eager to please, though lately he's been mesmerized by the satisfying symmetry of the elastic straps that cut across the back of Tanya, who sits in front of him. He has noticed that Tanya rotates among three different bras, and that on one of these bras, the lower hook is broken. Dobrin thinks that Lana from TV would never wear a bra with a broken hook, and yet he's realistic that his possibilities for any type of contact are much greater with Tanya than they are with Lana. And in this bra Tanya is one step closer to being unclothed. Lately he's been devising strategies to increase their contact, the key strategy being to stand as close to Tanya's desk as possible while he stacks his books or puts on his coat. As of yet, she's only hit him with her elbow.

"Dobrin!" Kuneva is standing over his desk, looking at his half-finished homework.

Dobrin looks at it too, with more disappointment than guilt: he wishes it were done. The night before, he had sat down with his workbook in front of the TV. His goal was to have the homework finished by halftime. But the game wasn't so interesting because it was a replay of a game they'd seen before, and Dobrin got to thinking about other things, namely his father and the fact that he had not spoken to Dobrin in an awfully long time. He started to wonder if maybe Tatko was angry at him, too, and once that thought got stuck in his mind, it became very important to say something, though he didn't know what. The goal became finding something to say by halftime, and this was all Dobrin could think about until moments before the buzzer, when he finally blurted out, "Who do you want to win?" Which was a stupid question of course because they had seen the game, and they knew who would win.

After all that, Dobrin was relieved when Tatko ignored him.

In the corner of his mind, Dobrin registers Stassi talking, something about a date with Lana. On the homework sheet lying on his desk, he sees that he quit writing in the middle of a word.

"Dobrine," Kuneva exhales in her weary way, "You have so much potential." For once, Dobrin is not fooled.

Maika wants to make one more trip to the garden to gather vegetables for the winter, and would anyone like to come. The way she says it, it's clear Dobrin is supposed to join her.

Every spring, Maika plants *tomati*, peppers, onions, garlic, potatoes, pumpkins and zucchini—twice as much as she needs because half will fail from slugs or neglect. Maika doesn't have time to care for the garden. The untended fruit rots on the ground. As it is, they have not been to the garden in more than a month, not since the day of the satellite TV. Dobrin is not eager to go. The slugs will be all over everything, and he will spend the entire time collecting them in a jar. This late in the season, they will be the size of chili peppers.

But what Dobrin wants is irrelevant. His mother's migraine has subsided for the first time in a long while, reason enough for him to go. And there's the incident that happened last night.

Maika had gone to bed. Stassi had stayed late watching TV and comparing every girl to his father's girlfriend. "You think *she's* got hooters!" he said, using a word he'd learned from an American film. Stassi could pick things up just like that. "You haven't *seen* hooters until you've seen my father's girlfriend."

"*Kakvo e dumata?*" Tatko said. "Hoo-ters?" Stassi sniggered at his strained pronunciation of the word. "Hoo-ters," Tatko said again, and Stassi clapped his hands.

They'd barely heard Maika's shuffling outside the door, barely turned the channel in time, and when they did, they flipped to a news program that Maika surely knew they had not been watching.

"What's so funny?" Maika said to Dobrin. Stassi was bent in half, shaking with laughter, and Tatko was smirking.

"*Nishto*," Dobrin scowled. Indeed, there was nothing funny about it: his father grinning like a schoolboy, his mother standing there in a nightgown too worn for company to see. Dobrin wished he could buy her a new robe and maybe a new haircut. He wondered if a new tube of lipstick could turn her lips into a smile.

The road to the garden is lined with houses; usually it takes a long time to get there because Maika has to talk to everyone. But this day they walk straight up the mountain. The first half of the walk is a paved road, which they manage easily. But when the road turns to dirt, Maika's shoes slip on the wet ground and gather a thick rim of mud around the edges. Dobrin keeps his hand on her back to steady her.

When they reach the garden, Dobrin takes the jar Maika hands him and starts collecting the slugs. It is cool enough that the flies are gone, and the air is sweet with the rich ferment of composting fruit. Dobrin finds a sturdy twig about a foot long and starts picking the slugs off the pumpkins and zucchini that are still good. While Dobrin collects slugs, Maika rakes fiercely at the rotting tomatoes and cucumbers, combing them into a heap in a corner of the plot. Even though they are at opposite ends of the garden, he can feel the soft thud of her rake hitting the soil.

Dobrin tries to imagine Tanya working in the garden. Wondering what she'd wear, he keeps coming back to her snug green turtleneck, not only because it looks very nice on her, but also because of the green vegetation, and he thinks it would be a good match. He imagines her picking strawberries and tomatoes and cucumbers in peak condition. He doubts very much that Tanya has ever seen a slug.

Maika has finished raking and is coming up behind him, choosing the squashes to take home and wiping them with a dirty towel. "Dobrin*e*," she says. "I want you to be a good boy, you hear?"

It has been a long time since Dobrin's mother reminded him to be a good boy. She used to tell him this all the time. "Be a good boy at school today," she'd say. "Be a good boy and clear off the table." If Tatko heard her say this, he would mock her. "That's right, Dobrin*e*. You be a good boy," he would say, and Dobrin could tell he did not really mean it. Dobrin would not know what to do, who to please—usually his mother because he wanted to make her happy.

There in the garden, the words *Be a good boy* sound hollow as a rotted-out squash. Dobrin does not know what a good boy is, let alone how to be one.

At two months, Stassi says there's still a chance. He says even if you don't like a person, if you share the same bed with them night after night, eventually you will have sex.

It's just a matter of time. Only yesterday Dobrin had thought his parents were on the verge of a breakthrough. The prices for central heat had finally been taped to the post office windows. They were impossibly high, higher than they had ever been. Maika figured they could afford to heat only two rooms, the living room and one other. She said it should be Dobrin's room; he was not the one who got them into this situation.

"*Gluposti,*" Tatko said, staring hard at the TV. "Dobrin's room is the smallest."

In the seconds that Maika took to formulate her response, Dobrin had felt them on the edge of a conversation. Oh, this would be good! A fight, even one that all the neighbors could hear, would be better than so much quiet.

But Maika had turned things in another direction. "Fine then," she said. To Dobrin she added, "You sleep with me, and your father will sleep on the couch."

Tatko snorted. He has been on the couch ever since the satellite TV was installed.

"I like the cold," Dobrin said. He did not want to sleep with his mother. But Maika was clattering dishes in the cabinet; Tatko was turning up the volume on the TV. "I like the cold," he said again, louder and more insistent, but no one seemed to notice.

When the border is approached, eyed, retreated from, this is when Dobrin feels most discouraged. "There's still hope, bro," Stassi says. Dobrin hates it when Stassi calls him *bro.*

Cold is cumulative, Dobrin decides as he lies awake in bed. Two weeks of trying to beat the cold and he is losing the battle. It is only the end of November; he has at least four months of cold, freezing cold, ahead of him. He has taken to showering before he sleeps, starting the night out with groundless optimism: tonight he will be warm! But by two, three o'clock, any heat he started out with has escaped through the weave of the layered Rhodope blankets and dissolved into the air. Moment to moment, he tracks the steady creep of the chill as it penetrates his toes, feet, and ankles, loitering in his bones. He pulls the covers over his head to capture the warmth of his breath. It is a marvel to him that such warm air can come from such a cold body.

Even with his head beneath the blankets, he can hear the satellite TV. Listening to Tatko flip from the girls to a basketball match, he is tempted to go watch a quarter and warm up, but he doesn't particularly feel like being with his father right now.

Earlier that evening, Maika had sent Tatko out on what should have been a quick errand. "Dobrine, tell your father to go buy bread," she'd said. Tatko had not returned until long after dinner was finished. Dobrin and Maika had eaten alone, *gyuveche* with no bread, no satellite TV. Amidst so much stillness, Dobrin felt small pinches of anger at the cat, who did none of his usual mewing for food from the table but curled up in a ball in the dent Tatko left on the couch; at the radiator, which did not hiss and pop as it so often did, but purred quietly without any punctuation whatsoever; and at his mother, whose bites slowed to a stop with half her dinner uneaten. That was one thing about the satellite TV. Rarely did it pause between commercials and programs, and never, *never* did it stop.

Lately, Dobrin has started to wonder if they will go on forever like this, the quiet getting quieter, togetherness growing strained and unyielding, until things are impossibly hard, a fossilized existence. Beneath the layers of blankets, cold, anger, he lies still, like a body entombed. After a while, he bends a leg beneath the covers to make sure he can.

When Dobrin finally climbs into bed with his mother, he does it in the middle of the night, when his father is dozing in front of the TV, his face awash with electronic color. Dobrin's skin is chapped from the moisture of his breath beneath the covers. His nose is running. He opens and closes doors quietly. Once he has closed his mother's door behind him, he stands still, waiting for his eyes to adjust.

The room smells of Vilichka's herbs, and the radiator crackles. Even though his mother is all the way over to one side of the bed—it's clear she's been expecting him—her heat is everywhere under the covers. Cold though he is, Dobrin finds this disgusting. He wonders how he was ever able to sleep with his mother when he was a child. He can hardly bring himself to get in the bed, and once he does, he lies stiffly on the edge. He is awake and acutely aware of the thawing in his fingers and toes.

Stassi crosses a line when he claims his dad's girlfriend is even hotter than Lana. "She's from Germany," he says to Dobrin on a break between classes. Neither of them has pocket money to spend in the café, so they stay in the classroom, which stinks of damp chalk and body odor.

Dobrin leans against the radiator, pressing his fingers into its grooves. "So what?" He is tired of hearing about Stassi's father. Stassi's father lives in a huge apartment in Sofia. Stassi's father takes him to soccer matches. Stassi's father eats dinner at McDonald's almost every night. Dobrin thinks that if Stassi's father was so great, he might visit every once in a while.

"So she's pretty."

"Being German doesn't necessarily make you pretty," Dobrin says. There is a German teacher at school who isn't pretty at all.

"This one is. And she has real blonde hair. My dad says she's blonde *everywhere*."

Dobrin tries to imagine how this might come up in conversation between Stassi and his father. He doesn't think his own father would share such a detail. Besides, what about armpits? So many summers at the pool, and Dobrin has yet to see a pit that is blonde. "You lie," he says, though he is not sure about this. He is not sure of anything Stassi says anymore.

He feels his mood deteriorating. The day started out well. He had done his homework and received a good mark. He asked Tanya for a pencil, and she turned around and offered him a choice of implements. Dobrin took his time deliberating and had gotten a good look at the rounded silhouette of her breast. For a small girl, she has big hooters.

The class is starting to file back in. Dobrin is glad that the break is almost over and Stassi will have to return to his seat.

"Anyhow, tell your dad the answer is yes."

"Yes, what?"

"Yes on the German girlfriend. My dad can hook him up."

Stassi waits for Dobrin's face to turn hot before he breaks into one of his cackles. "I got you, bro," he screams, stomping his feet on the ground.

Dobrin has wanted to punch Stassi for a long time. Mrs. Kuneva gets there just in time to see his fist land squarely in Stassi's eye.

A week of sleeping in Maika's bed and Dobrin has learned that if he can distract himself from the intense heat under the covers and the smell of Vilichka's herbs, he eventually will fall asleep. He strains to hear the score of the game, but all he can make out is the rush of the crowd, which, when filtered through the bedroom wall, sounds like running water.

In less than a month they will be into the new year and on the down-hill slope toward summer. Dobrin has been thinking that next summer he wants to be a real lifeguard, which means he will need training and a new bathing suit. When the winter is over and Maika is no longer paying for heat, he will ask her if she can afford these things. If everything works out, when Vulkov pays him at the end of the summer, Dobrin will be able to pay her back.

Payback. They are just now studying compound words. Cutthroat. Diehard. Kuneva makes the mistake of defining payback as *tit for tat*. Stassi has never heard anything so wonderful.

Tit for tat, he says about the punch. "Don't worry about it, bro," which makes Dobrin want to punch him again, if Stassi wouldn't like it so much. Stassi is infatuated with the ring of purple that encircles his eye. He spends the whole class touching it. On breaks, he goes to the bathroom to see if it has changed. Kuneva has decided that for as long as the bruise lasts, Dobrin must stay after school each day and write a one-page essay. The first day she made him write on the meaning of friendship. The second day he had to come up with different ways of working things out.

In bed next to him, Maika rolls from her back onto her side. When his mother lies this way, Dobrin thinks her torso looks like an angry violin. He can remember a time when things didn't always end in anger, when near arguments—those crackling moments when there's still a choice about which way things can go—ended with Tatko pulling Maika onto his lap and wrapping his arms around her waist, nuzzling her with his big, oily nose. Maika would laugh—*stiga be! that tickles!*—and Dobrin would laugh too. Tatko might find her breast with his hand and hold it for a moment before she pulled away. That was years ago, and still Dobrin can remember how he felt, at once joyous and bashful. Maika would extract herself from Tatko's grasp, and Tatko would stare after her—her chest or her retreating behind—the way he now stares at the girls on the satellite TV.

Love? Lust? Only now is Dobrin starting to suspect there is a difference. When he is watching the satellite TV, it is easy to believe he loves Lana and all her sprawling beauty. He loves the way she makes him feel. But during the daytime, he thinks that what he feels for Lana is something less than love. He is not sure why he thinks this, only that there must be something more to it than the sensations she ignites in his groin. He thinks of all the silly hearts he used to draw for Maika. *C lubov, Dobrin.* From Dobrin with love.

Earlier that day, Tanya paid him a compliment.

"I like your sweater," she said, not looking at him but playing with the zipper on her rucksack.

"You do?" Dobrin had only two sweaters, a blue one and a brown one, both knit by his *baba* and inherited from his father, both ugly and old and smelling of cedar. What was there to like about such sweaters? Dobrin was wearing the brown one. He could see the ends of the yarn poking through the weave at the places where his grandma had finished one ball and started the next. He hated this sweater. Nevertheless, he wore it because the chill was still there—he could not get past it. This sweater was the warmest piece of clothing he had.

Tanya turned in her chair, and he could see he had embarrassed her. He scrambled for something to say to fix things. "Thank you." Or "It's old." Or "I like your sweater, too," which he actually did. Oh, God, he did. It was pink, starting to gray with age, and a little too small. Depending on the way she sat, the sweater rode up in the back, showing off an oval of bright white skin. It seemed terribly intimate to Dobrin that he should see this skin so low on her back, perfectly creased by the faint ridge of her spine. He wondered if she knew about this skin, if maybe she wanted him to see it.

Dobrin can hear the match on the satellite TV. That afternoon Stassi had asked to come over to watch it, but Dobrin had told him no.

That exchange had taken place after school, after Dobrin's detention, during which Kuneva had made him write an essay on ways to keep warm during the winter months. Of his own volition, Stassi had waited for Dobrin out in the hall, periodically kicking his soccer ball at the door to remind Dobrin he was still there. Dobrin had taken his time, hoping that Kuneva would yell at Stassi and make him go home, but she just sat there, writing marks in the *Dnevnika*. More than once Dobrin saw her pen skip when the ball slammed against the door, but surprisingly she held her temper.

"What do you mean, *no?*" Stassi said. "Barcelona, bro! Aren't you going to watch?"

Dobrin had planned on watching the match, but then he changed his mind. "My parents said they want a night with just our family."

"What do you mean?" Stassi said, fingering the mottled ring around his eye. "They're talking again?"

"A little." Dobrin had not intended to tell this lie, but he was happy with how it sounded. He wondered if it even was a lie, or if it could be true. Maybe things *were* getting better, and he was just not seeing it.

"Didn't I tell you?" Stassi said, trying to maintain his cheer—but Dobrin could tell he was mad. "*Ami*, fine," he said, kicking the ball down the stairs and running after it. Dobrin followed at a slower pace. When he got outside, Stassi was nowhere in sight.

Now Dobrin can hear the satellite TV switch from the game back to the girls, the familiar music, always the same music, filtering through the wall. He slips his hand inside his underwear and inhales softly.

He had not said anything to Tanya after the sweater incident. She had not given him the chance. After class she had practically run from the room, leaving Dobrin to wonder if she was embarrassed or hurt or just in a hurry. Several times he's questioned if the moment really happened, if she said anything to him at all. Tomorrow he will redeem himself. He will say something to her whether or not he has a reason. He will find something. He will tell her he likes her rucksack or her nibbled pencils or the slope of her back when she leans forward over her desk. He will tell her that over the summer he had noticed her tan lines and the way her bathing suit rode up over her hips. He will wear his brown sweater, and Tanya—oh, Tanya. He will ask her if she wants to come over and watch a show on the satellite TV. She can choose the program. She can. Oh. There in the darkness, it seems so easy. The million things he would like to tell her. Yes.

With one swift movement, Maika throws back her covers and rises from the bed. Dobrin uses his clean hand to cover his face and waits the humiliating stretch of time as she fumbles for her slippers, her sweater, the doorknob. He hears the kitchen door open and close, listens to the tick of the gas turning on, the oven door opening, the chair pulled up close.

This is how they will spend the night. Maika in front of the oven, Tatko in front of the satellite TV and Dobrin in a puddle of his own misery, wondering if this is how it feels to be a man.

Cynthia Morrison Phoel graduated from the Warren Wilson College MFA Program for Writers in 2003. She lives in Boston, where she is working on a collection of stories set in Bulgaria. This is her first published story.

BERNARD JR.'S UNCLE LUSCIOUS/
Emily Raboteau

WE DON'T WANNA GO," the boys said at the same time. It was the first Saturday of the summer, and they were salting a slug under the pecan tree out back.

Nanan Zanobia adjusted her pillbox hat. "What you mean you don't wanna go?" she asked, pointing her eyes at B. J., who was short, serious and round as a potato. "I know I don't have to remind you she's your mother." Then she pointed her eyes at Luscious, who was long, pretty and thin as a string bean. "And I know I don't have to remind you she's your sister." Nobody knew just how old Nan Zan was or how many other people's children she'd raised, but everyone agreed she had scary eyes. Her face was dark as a chestnut, but her irises were so light blue they were almost white. "Or am I gonna have to remind you with a switch from this tree?"

"No, ma'am," said B. J., looking down at his corrective shoe. For most of his early childhood he'd worn a brace on his right leg, which had been twisted inward at birth, and he still walked with a limp.

"But Nan, I'm supposed to help out Miss Pauline at the Curly-Q today," whined Luscious. He had a slight lisp and was rumored to be a pansy.

"You got a summerful of Sairdays to be Miss Pauline's shampoo boy. Today you're going to visit your sister up at the hospital and stop giving me lip, hear?"

Luscious looked down at the place in front of his bare feet where the salted slug was turning inside out like the wrong side of an eyelid.

"Good Lord. Is that one of God's creatures?"

"Yes, ma'am," answered B. J., pushing up on the bridge of his glasses, although they hadn't slipped down his nose. The slug was writhing and oozing in the dust, like a rabid tongue.

"What I tell you two about tormenting animals?"

"It's just a bug," mumbled Luscious, rolling his eyes.

"What I tell you?"

"Do unto others," they said at the same time.

"That's right. Everybody 'just a bug' to someone else who think they bigger and better. That don't mean they a bug. It mean someone else got a problem with they eyes. Now get in the house, wash up and throw on your Sunday clothes. We got a bus to catch."

"I don't care what she says. A slug is a bug," Luscious said under his breath as they trudged past the chicken coop toward the back of the shotgun shack, up the sagging porch, through the kitchen and into the airless boxcar of a room they shared.

Luscious had lived there since he was a baby, when his mama ran off to Chicago to sing in a nightclub and got herself stabbed on Blackhawk Street. Bernard had lived there since the age of three, when his mama finally lost her mind at the five and dime after trying twice to drown herself in the Gulf of Mexico and once to slice her wrists with the lid of a peach can. People still talked about it. How she had pushed over one shelf with a half a ton of merchandise onto the one behind it and how all the shelves toppled down in slow motion like a line of dominoes, the last one shattering the storefront window and disfiguring Dudley, the waterhead man, who was sweeping the sidewalk out front. Nobody blamed her after what she'd been through, but everyone agreed with the judge's order when he sent her over to Biloxi to get her head straightened out.

"And if that place is a hospital then my name's Dwight D. Eisenhower."

"Shhh," whispered B. J. "She can still hear you."

The boys were twelve and thirteen now. Even though Luscious was only eight months older, he insisted that B. J. call him "Uncle."

"Miss Pauline was gon' pay me fitty cents for washing heads, too."

"Hush, Uncle Luscious. She'll hear you."

"So what if she do? Shoot. That's good hard-earned money I'm losing. How'm I supposed to buy a guitar when I gotta go to the nuthouse on my workday? Look at this thing." He held up a shoebox with rubber bands stretched over the top and plucked at it. It made a twangy sound that rose up at the end like a question. "You ever see a sorrier instrument than this here?"

B. J. shrugged his shoulders and struggled into the pants of his hand-me-down baby blue Sunday suit. Luscious had grown out of it the year before. Nan Zan had taken up the cuffs of the jacket and pants and let out the waist to fit over B. J.'s belly. The suit was shiny in the spots where Luscious's elbows and knees had worn it thin, but those spots fell somewhere below B. J.'s elbows and knees.

"That old woman's got it in for me. I swear."

"I dunno."

"What you mean you dunno?"

"I mean she has a point is all."

"No she don't."

"Yes she do."

"No she don't."

"Yes she do."

"What's her point then?"

"How she's your big sister and all."

"Half-sister. And she's your crazy mama. So what?" Luscious looked haphazardly through the chest under their bunkbed.

"So we're her family. She's expecting us."

Luscious sucked his teeth. "She don't remember either one of us. Or Nan. Why can't I find my pants? Didn't Sarah just sit there staring at the floor last time?"

B. J. didn't say anything.

"Here they go. Yes she did. Just sat there shimmying her leg and staring at the floor like a zombie. She didn't even look at those Easter eggs we brung her."

"Don't say that."

"Why not? It's the truth. Besides, you just got done telling Nan you didn't want to go any more than me. Where's my goddamned Sunday shirt?"

"Shhh. In Nan's wardrobe. She ironed it for you."

Luscious strode into the room railroaded behind theirs. B. J. clipped on his tie and followed his uncle. Nan's room was almost entirely taken up by a four-poster bed. Above the bed hung a wooden crucifix with a pewter Jesus nailed to it. You could see all of his ribs and the muscles in his stomach. Around the crucifix hung close to two dozen hand-tinted photos of children Nan had brought up. One of them was a dentist now. One of them was a mayor. One of them was B. J.'s daddy. In the picture he looked to be about eighteen years old. He had posed with a baseball bat, crouched in batting stance, smiling into the sun. The picture was blurry, as if the person snapping the shot had forgotten to focus the lens, but you could still see how white his teeth were.

B. J. sat on the bed and pulled at a loose thread in the patchwork quilt. "I don't mind the nuthouse," he said, which was a baldfaced lie because he was terrified of the nuthouse.

"Bullshit. I don't see it in here." The open wardrobe smelled like mothballs and mildew.

"Hanging next to Nan's raincoat."

"Oh." Luscious stuck his long arms into the sleeves of his starched shirt and buttoned it. He checked himself out in the mirror on the inside of the wardrobe door. The mirror was cloudy and freckled, not because it was dirty but because it was ancient. "I look gooood, don't I?"

"You look awright."

Luscious whistled at his reflection. "I am one pretty nigger," he said. "Too bad I got to waste it on a bunch of basket cases." He looked at B. J. "Hey, you look nice too."

"Thanks."

"Sorry I called your Mama a crazy zombie."

Pretty much all the white folks on the bus were going to Biloxi to visit someone in prison. Nan Zan and the boys boarded and were making their way down the aisle to the back when a little white boy stuck out his foot. B. J. tripped, lost hold of the library book he'd been carrying and fell flat on his face. Several people snickered.

"Jasper John!" said the little boy's mother. She had so much makeup on her face that she looked like a clown. "Did you just do what I think you did?"

Nan stopped to give B. J. a hand.

"Step to the back, auntie," called the bus driver.

"Did you just trip him?"

"No, Ma."

"Don't you fib."

"He fell on his own. See?" He pointed at B. J.'s corrective shoe. "He's a cripple."

"You oughta be ashamed."

"What for?"

"For acting up, that's what. If your father was here, he'd smack you silly."

B. J. adjusted his glasses, which had slipped off. He blinked his eyes. He saw his library book under a seat and reached for it. A foot kicked it, and it slid back under the next seat, too far for him to reach. Someone giggled above him. He crawled toward the book and reached for it again. Another foot stomped down on the back of his hand and twisted, hard, like it was putting out a cigarette. B. J. yanked his hand free, grabbed his book and pushed himself up. His hand throbbed. So did his chin, from where it had struck the floor of the bus.

"Just say you're sorry to the poor colored boy."

"I'm sorry to the poor fat colored boy," said Jasper John, looking at the ceiling of the bus.

"I swear, if your father was here—"

"Well he ain't," said Jasper John, crossing his arms, "so shut your pie hole."

His mother smacked him.

B. J. sucked in his stomach, limped to the back of the bus and sat next to Nan Zan. *"Cracker trash,"* Luscious said under his breath. "You awright?" he asked. A muscle under his eye twitched.

"Yeah."

Nan Zan straightened B. J.'s jacket. "Lord have mercy, would you look at this," she muttered. Someone's chewing gum had stuck to one of the lapels. She pulled a napkin out of the pail on her lap and dabbed at it. The gum was sticky and had melted in the heat. It stretched out like a tightrope. She scraped at it with her hat pin, but a pink spot remained. "I'll get the rest out later with some salt, honeylamb," she said.

"Okay."

B. J. opened his library book. It was *Oliver Twist*, and several pages were missing, but he liked it anyway because it was about an orphan. He was only allowed to check one book out of the bookmobile at a time. In one week he had already read *Oliver Twist* twice, and another week would pass before the bookmobile came around again on its summer schedule. He stared at what someone had scrawled on the inside cover in pencil. The words blurred up so he couldn't make them out, but he remembered what they said: "Gracie Champlain is a Grade A slut." He turned to the first page. His hands were shaking, and his face was hot.

"Look at me, Bernard Jr." Nan Zan took his chin in her hand. She wet her thumb with her tongue and rubbed away the streak of dirt on his cheek. She looked at his face. "I'm *so* proud of you."

"I know," he said.

It smelled like a zoo in the east wing. Most of the patients were tied to their bed frames. One of them screamed somewhere, and the sound reverberated against the mint green walls. Then someone else screamed. This reminded B. J. of birdcall. He couldn't tell where exactly the screaming was coming from.

There were four patients to a room, and none of the rooms had doors. B. J. tried not to look, but Luscious was staring. It was difficult to tell the men from the women except for a couple of individuals who were naked. Everyone else wore standard-issue white cotton pajamas and white ankle socks. Some of the patients were bleeding at the ankles and wrists where their restraints had rubbed them raw, and some of them had soiled themselves, and some of them had shaved heads, and some of them were veterans who had lost limbs or eyes in the War.

One man was missing both his legs. They'd been amputated above his hips. He was propped up against his headboard, sitting on his pillow, and when the boys passed his room he stretched out his arms and pretended to shoot bullets at them through his pointer fingers. Luscious told B. J. he bet they'd cut off that man's pecker, judging from where his body ended, and he probably wore a garbage bag for underpants to catch his mess.

"Maybe so," said B. J.

They were lagging behind Nan and the Assistant Director, who led them down the long hallway.

"Why did you move her to this wing?" Nan asked.

"She had an episode, and we thought she'd be better off here," said the Assistant Director. He wore a white coat and carried a clipboard.

"What happened?" asked Nan.

"We took care of it, and she's doing much better now."

"Well, when do you expect to move her back to the north wing?"

"That depends on several factors. Here we are." He looked at his clipboard, stepped into the doorway and called to the woman in the second bed from the left, "Sarah, your folks are here."

The woman turned her head to them. She was thirty-one years old, and her hair was completely white. The bed sheet was pulled up to her armpits. It was also white. Her face was pretty and looked a little like both of the boys', although neither one of them resembled the other. There was a bandage on the side of her neck. She turned her head away.

"Good Lord," said Nan. "What happened to her neck?"

"That's self inflicted. Please try not to excite her and don't undo the restraints. That's just a precaution so she won't hurt herself again."

Nan and the boys stepped over to Sarah's bed. There weren't any chairs in the room, so they stood there. The room smelled vaguely anti-septic.

"I just don't understand this," said Nan.

"Remember to sign out at the front on your way out," called the Assistant Director. Then he was gone.

Nan handed her pail to Luscious. "Hey there, Sarah," she said sitting at the top of the bed. "Do these hurt?" She started to untie the restraints.

"Don't," blurted B. J. "She might hurt herself."

"I'll just loosen them a little to make her more comfortable. Look, Sarah. I brought your baby brother. Say hello, Luscious."

"Hey, Sarah. How you makin' it?"

"And here's your son. Give your mama a kiss, Bernard Jr."

"In a minute."

"Look how much he's grown since Easter. Everybody says he's the spitting image of his daddy. Just a little more hefty. Tell her your good news, sugar."

"You tell her."

"Bernard Jr. here won himself a scholarship to a fancy boys' school up in New Orleans. He'll be moving up there end of August so he can start in September. This the last time you'll see him before he shoves off. It's a Catholic boarding school. They say he so smart they gon' skip him two grades and put him in the high school. They gon' take up a collection for him at St. Rose de Lima, too, for the school uniform and all those books he gonna need."

"And I got a job at the Curly-Q," added Luscious.

Nan Zan stroked Sarah's hair. "When's the last time they combed your hair, sugarpie? I should have brought my comb."

A dry noise came from Sarah's throat.

"What's that, Sarah? Is there something you need, honey? Bring me that pail, Luscious."

Luscious stepped forward with the pail.

"If you're hungry, I brought you some fried shrimp and some pound cake and some sweet peas from my garden. If you're thirsty, I have lemonade. Bernard Jr. squeezed the lemons for me."

"I'm hungry!" announced the woman in the first bed. "I'm *starving*." She had two depressions in her forehead, as if someone had scooped two spoonfulls out of a mound of dough. Her head was covered with gray stubble, and she had whiskers on her chin.

"Well, we got plenty to go around," said Nan, standing up and smoothing her dress. "I'm gonna go see if I can't talk to the Director about all this and get some new dressing for that neck wound. Luscious, bring the lady some shrimp. I'll be back soon."

"Her hands are tied," said Luscious.

"You can feed me," the woman said. "I won't bite."

Luscious went over with the pail. Nan went to find the director. B. J. sat where Nan had been at the head of the bed and looked at the side of his mother's face, which was turned away from him. He looked at her ear. It was filled with rust-colored wax. He looked at the bandage on her neck. It was dirty.

"Hey, Mama," he said.

"Just drop it in my mouth, boy," instructed the woman in the first bed. "I still have all my teeth. See?" She bared her teeth. They were yellow and stained.

Luscious started feeding her shrimp.

"Delicious," she said with her mouth full. "Much obliged."

"Nan made it. She's a good cook."

"I'll say. She your granny?"

"Nan? Naw, she's my—she's just Nan."

My Granny was a hooker in New Orleans . . ." sang the woman. "You know that little ditty?"

"Never did hear that one."

"That's 'cause I just now made it up."

"Too bad I didn't bring my guitar," said Luscious. "We could have played a duet. More shrimp?"

"You bet, sonny." She smacked her lips. "I notice you're staring at my noggin."

"Oh . . . pardon."

"No need for apologies. You wanna know why it look the way it do?"

She lowered her voice. "They interfered with my brain and took out my memory."

Luscious looked at B. J. B. J. looked at Luscious. Luscious looked back at the woman. "Did it hurt much?"

"I can't remember."

"I'm sorry."

"Don't be. Worse things have happened. They could have taken my heart. Or my intestines. Oh, they take any old body part they please and run scientific experiments on 'em. Liver, kidneys, stomach, what-have-you. I've seen it done more times than I care to speak of. More shrimp, please."

"I think I better save the rest for Sarah," Luscious said, although B. J. wound up eating the remaining shrimp on the long bus ride home, one after the other, without hardly chewing.

"Suit yourself. It's real good of you to come visit your mama."

"She's not my mama. She's my half-sister. We got the same daddy."

"I see. She's a awright roommate for a colored girl. She's better than them two chowderheads," she said, referring to the women in beds three and four, both of whom appeared comatose and were drooling. "I like your sister, but she don't say much."

"Oh, she don't talk at all. She stopped speaking altogether when she lost her mind at the five and dime."

"That ain't true. She said something just last night."

"What'd she say?" B. J. piped in.

"Sounded like she said, 'Steal home.'"

"Steal home?" asked B. J.

"I believe that's what she said. She won't say it again, though. They went in and took her throat."

"Look at me, Mama," said B. J.

Sarah arched her back then and screamed. It was a long scream that echoed off the walls and was answered by someone down the hall.

"What do you think she meant?" asked B. J. They were lying in the shade of the pecan tree. B. J. was finishing *Oliver Twist* for the third time. He had a bruise on his chin and on the back of his hand. Luscious was picking out a song on his shoebox guitar. He had a cut on his finger. The sun was going down, but it was still hot.

"Huh?"

"Steal home. I figure she might have been talking 'bout my daddy."

"Since he played baseball and all?"

Almost everything B. J. knew about his daddy was from the old men at Benoit's Barbershop. Those men still talked about Bernard Boudroux's potential batting average like it was legend. From what B. J. had gathered, his daddy had everything going for him before he died. He had just married Sarah, worked a good job managing the icehouse at night and had been visited by a scout from the Negro American League when he was killed. Nobody would talk about how it happened.

"That story's too ugly to pass on," Nan Zan would say, "but it had a happy ending, and that's you." B. J. had been born premature, two weeks on the heels of his daddy's death.

He tried to assemble snatches of information about his parents in a way that would explain what had gone wrong. He couldn't remember much about his mama except talcum powder on her breasts and hiding under her skirt. People said she'd been a remarkable beauty, that a white traveling life insurance salesman from San Francisco had asked her to marry him when she was just sixteen. So had Moe Haskell, who ran the colored funeral home, but she only had eyes for his daddy, they said. B. J. always imagined that something bad had gone down at the icehouse, that his daddy had been killed in that place, possibly crushed by a block of ice, as by an elephant.

The barbershop stories were clues that pricked his ears. King Benoit would start, while conking somebody's head to look like Nat King Cole. "Your daddy was some strongman slugger. He coulda been the next Turkey Stearnes."

"He coulda been better than Turkey Stearnes. He coulda been the next Josh Gibson," Oscar Brown or somebody else playing checkers in the corner would add. "When he was in high school, your daddy batted .351."

"One year your daddy hit fifty-four home runs."

"Fifty-nine."

"And he was fast."

"Lord almighty, he was fast."

"We called him the Iceman."

"Your daddy could go from first to third on a bunt."

"He could steal two bases on one pitch."

"Once he hit a single up the middle and got hit by the same ball he batted when he slid into second."

"Your daddy was so fast he could cut off the light and hop into bed before the room went dark."

Then they would start running off stories about Cool Papa Bell and Smokey Joe Williams and especially Satchell Paige. B. J. would get these stories confused in his mind. He'd look up at the picture of Jackie Robinson over the barbershop sink and halfway think it was his daddy.

"It's a shame what happened to your daddy," someone would finish, picking up the *Jet* magazine they had left off reading to talk about baseball. The room would grow reverently silent then, until the man in the barber chair would clear his throat and complain about the job King was doing on his head.

Hearing these stories made B. J. more sad than proud. He had no aptitude for sports on account of his leg and could never follow in his father's shoes. He sensed he was a disappointment to the old men.

He thought about what his mama meant by "Steal home," if it was a message or a clue. Through the leaves of the pecan tree, the sky was now the color of the inside of a peach. The katydids were singing in the grass. *Katy-did, Katy-didn't, Katy-did.*

"I'm bored," said Luscious. "Let's go gig a frog or somethin'."

The summer wore on. The days spun out like one long endless day. On Sundays they sat through mass at St. Rose de Lima and lit candles for Sarah. On Saturdays Luscious washed heads at the Curly-Q. Every other Friday the bookmobile rolled around and B. J. borrowed a book. They listened to the radio. They helped Nan weed her garden, bordered by sun-bleached seashells. They tortured small animals and insects. They swam in the bay. They avoided talking about how B. J. was going to leave when the summer was up.

One day in July they were lying out back when a cricket jumped from Nan's patch of black-eyed Susans and landed near B. J.'s head. He quickly cupped his hand over it. It tickled his palm.

"I got a cricket," said B. J.

"Rip off her wings and legs. No! How 'bout leave one leg on her and set her down."

"Awright." B. J. was methodical about yanking her apart. He lined up her wings and legs on top of his library book, *On Walden Pond*. Then he dropped her in the dirt, where she twitched around in a circle with her one remaining leg.

"Go, Fat Sally, go," said Luscious. The boys leaned on their elbows and watched. Eventually she stopped moving.

"Gimme your glasses," said Luscious.

Luscious caught the sun in one of the lenses and aimed it at the bug. She began to struggle in the hot pinpoint of light.

"Time me."

"One Miss'ippi, two Miss'ippi, three Miss'ippi, four Miss'ippi, five Miss'ippi, six Miss'ippi, seven Miss'ippi, eight Miss'ippi, nine Miss'-ippi . . ." B. J. thought about the words "steal home"—how when you put the two words together it meant running into base when the other team wasn't looking and probably sliding and getting dirt on your pants and cheering and pats on the back from your teammates if you made it, but also how in another way it could mean robbing someone of their house or their land, stealing it from them and making it yours and sending them packing like those Indians on the Trail of Tears, and how in a third way it sounded like steel home, a house made of steel, a bulletproof place for a superman to live . . . "forty-two Miss'ippi, forty-three Miss'ippi, forty-four Miss'ippi, forty-five Miss'ippi, forty-six Miss'ippi, forty-seven Miss'ippi, forty-eight Miss'ippi—"

"She's cooked," said Luscious. "What's the time?"

The cricket's body had turned black and shrunk.

"Forty-eight seconds."

"Almost beat my record."

"That's funny. I'm leaving in forty-eight days."

Luscious's expression changed. B. J. offered him the cricket legs.

"What I want them for? It's the wings make the song."

"I'm keeping her wings. I'm the one who caught her."

"Suit yourself, Shakespeare," said Luscious, chucking the glasses back at his nephew. They landed in the dirt next to the shriveled insect. B. J. picked them up, wiped them off on the bib of his overalls and put them back on.

"Don't call me that."

"Okay, *Shakespeare*."

"You mad or somethin'?"

"I'm bored." Luscious lay down like a corpse, with his arms folded over his chest, and closed his eyes. "Bored, bored, bored."

B. J. picked up the wings. They were impossibly light and veined like leaves. He stepped over his uncle and limped over to the back porch, under which the boys kept two cigar boxes full of feathers, claws, fur, shells, beaks and headless dragonflies. He added the wings to the box marked "B. J." He was hungry.

He could hear Nan Zan snoring inside even though she had her bedroom shutters closed to keep cool for her afternoon nap. Stepping as lightly as he could, he made his way up the porch steps and into the kitchen. He crept over to the icebox , snuck out the stick of butter, dipped it in the sugar bowl and bit into it like it was a candy bar.

"B. J.?" called Nan Zan from two rooms down. "That you in the butter?"

B. J. froze in his tracks and waited for the old woman's breathing to become regular again. Instead, she padded into the kitchen in her mules.

"I knew it. Keep your monkey paws off the butter, chile." She swiped it out of his hand and stuck it back in the icebox. "I'm expecting company tomorrow. I might just need that butter to whip up a cake. Don't you think a piece of chocolate cake on a plate would taste better than a stick of stolen butter?" She winked at him.

"Yes, ma'am."

"Now let an old lady catch a nap in peace."

"Nan?"

"What is it?"

"What do you think she meant?"

"Who?"

B. J.'s stomach growled. "Never mind."

Outside, Luscious was stretched out in the shade of the pecan tree, looking up and contemplating its leaves. B. J. rejoined him.

"I'm bored," said Luscious.

B. J. scratched his head. "I wish it was Friday already." The bookmobile was coming around that Friday. "I guess we could go down to the beach and watch the shrimp boats. Maybe take a dip."

"Awright. Ain't nothing better to do," said Luscious. "Grab our slingshots and let's go."

They walked along the train tracks in the direction of the bay.

"Hurry up, slowpoke," said Luscious.

"I'm looking for skipping stones," said B. J. He was out of breath. Soon they came upon the old icehouse. It had been unused for a few years, now that everyone had refrigerated iceboxes, and had fallen into a state of disrepair. Some of the planks had been stolen for lumber. Part of the roof had caved in. There were weeds and blackberry bushes growing out front like unkempt hair.

"There's the old icehouse," said Luscious.

"Yep," said B. J., looking down at his corrective shoe. The icehouse made him uneasy. He squatted down and picked up a stone that wasn't at all good for skipping and put it in his pocket.

"Looks like someone's movin' in."

There were several large wooden packing crates piled outside. Some of them were as tall as six feet. "Those look like coffins. Let's go peek," said Luscious.

"Naw."

"Don't you wanna know who's movin' in?"

"Not really."

"That place still give you the heebie-jeebies? Awright then. You just wait here a minute. I'm gonna go see what's what."

B. J. squatted down on the far side of the tracks with his back to the icehouse. It was high noon, and he was squatting on top of his own shadow. The heat was sitting low on the ground, making witchwater up and down the train tracks. He wrapped his arms around his knees and wished he'd brought his library book and wished he had some ice cream and wished his uncle would hurry up. He couldn't help imagining the inside of the icehouse, although he tried not to. He tried to think about *On Walden Pond* and the uniform he was going to wear to school in September, but his mind kept wandering to the icehouse behind him, not as it was now, decrepit and chewed on by termites, and not as he had ever known it to be, but as he imagined it had been when his father worked inside, hauling the bricks of ice and cutting off chunks of them with a pickax. Since he had only seen his daddy in the one photograph, the man he imagined was an amalgamation of men from movies and comic books and the barbershop stories, a man who walked like Jackie Robinson.

The icehouse in his mind was cool and damp inside, dark like St. Rose at nighttime. It sounded like a dripping faucet. The blocks of ice shone as if illuminated from within. They were heavy, and his father was tremendously strong to be able to lift them onto his shoulders. He imagined his father's muscles bulge as he picked at the ice with a motion of his arm like a blacksmith hammering steel. The Iceman. The ghost. With each blow, sparks of ice flew out like little filaments of fire. "Here," said Luscious. He thrust a handful of blackberries at B. J. "Nobody's there right now, but there's a cot up against the wall and a broom. Somebody's movin' in, that's for sure. I'll have another look-see on our way back."

The blackberries were overripe. B. J. tasted one. It was both too sour and too sweet at the same time. A needle of pain shot up through a small cavity in one of his molars and carried through his jaw to his ear canal. He spat into the dust between his knees, dropped the rest of the berries and stood up.

"What'd you go and do that for?" asked Luscious.

"I dunno."

"Ain't you hungry? You always hungry."

"I didn't want 'em. Let's go."

"Look!" said Luscious.

"What?"

"A inchworm." It was crawling out of one of the blackberries B. J. had dropped. It was the color of a new blade of grass.

"It's a tiny baby." B. J. reached out his hand to touch it.

Luscious slapped it away. "Nuh-uh. He's mine. I saw him first."

The inchworm lifted its front half and looked around to get its bearings. Then it started inching back in the direction of the icehouse.

"What you gon' do to him?"

"Let's see if he don't turn into two inchworms when I cut him in half."

"Awright."

Luscious dissected the inchworm with his thumbnail. Neither half moved or was consequential enough to keep.

They came to the road by the water, which was dark blue and spotted with foam. There were a few white people splashing there and a few more scattered on beach chairs under umbrellas to keep from getting sunburned. The sand was fine as sugar.

"Would you look at that," said Luscious. "They take up the whole beach and don't hardly use it."

They turned left on the beach road and walked three-quarters of a mile to the colored beach. It was rocky and packed with children. Further out, where the bay opened into the gulf, a fleet of shrimp boats bobbed in the water, dragging their nets beneath them.

The boys stripped down to their drawers and raced into the water, up to their necks. They dog-paddled past some little kids playing Marco Polo; then they dog-paddled toward the dock.

"Looks kinda crowded," said B. J. They came closer.

Gracie Champlain was sitting on the edge of the dock in her polka-dot two-piece, kicking her long brown legs. Purnell Jackson and the gang were surrounding her like buzzards, trying to convince her to jump in and take off her top underwater for a buffalo nickel. One of them hooked his finger under the strap across her back and snapped it. He had a hard-on.

"Hey," called Gracie, pointing at Luscious and B. J. "It's the little piggy and the big sissy." The boys on the dock laughed and slapped their thighs. Gracie heard them laughing and kept going. "We'd make room for y'all up here, but you stink." She wrinkled her nose.

"Shut up, Gracie," said Luscious.

"You gon' make me?"

"Let's go back," urged B. J. He was getting tired of treading water.

"You a pansy right? Ain't it true you don't like females?" Gracie asked.

"He likes girls," panted B. J., "just not your kind."

Gracie squinted her eyes. "What you mean, Porky Pig?"

"Word on the street is, you're a Grade A slut."

The gang laughed even harder at that.

Gracie stuck out her jaw. "What's so funny, Purnell?"

"Well, it's just—" he looked at his friends, "you gotta admit that's kinda true."

Gracie's face crumpled up. She stood and thumped down the dock toward the shore. The salt wind carried their laughter right behind her.

"First one to that buoy there gets my buffalo nickel," said Purnell, and they all canonballed into the water like hydrogen bombs.

Luscious and B. J. climbed up onto the dock.

B. J. lay on his back and looked at the clouds. He thought of his mother's hair. He was breathing heavily. Luscious sat at the edge, where Gracie had been, and looked out at the shrimp boats on the horizon. "She just jealous 'cause you're smarter than she is," he said. "And I'm prettier."

B. J. fell asleep for what felt like a long time, but when he woke up everything was the same. The little boys were still calling, "Marco!" "Polo." Luscious was still looking out at the boats. The clouds still looked like his mother's hair. Everything was a little blurry without his glasses, and the sun hurt his eyes. He closed them. "Uncle Luscious," he started, "when I go up to New Orleans—" Then he heard a splash, and a spray of water hit him. He opened his eyes and saw that his uncle had vanished.

"Look," said Luscious on the way back. There was a red pickup parked outside the icehouse, and all of the crates had apparently been taken inside, where it sounded like someone was hammering. "*Someone's here.*"

"Looks like it."

"How'm I supposed to see inside? They shut the door."

"You could knock."

"Are you crazy? That could be a ax murderer in there."

"You could peek through the cracks."

"I couldn't see nothing but his feet that way. Help me up on the roof. I'm gon' look in that hole."

B. J. looked up to the roof. There was a large crow sitting in the rain scuttle looking down at them. "I dunno about this."

"C'mon. Don't you wanna know who's in there?" Luscious crept around to the back of the icehouse. B. J. followed. "Lock your fingers together and gimme a boost. Yeah, like that. That's good." He grabbed the lip of the roof and lifted himself up. It wasn't difficult, since the icehouse was partly underground and the roof was low. As he started crawling toward the hole, the crow hopped over from the other side of the roof. It opened its wings and started squawking. With its wings open like that, it looked big as a dog.

"Shoo," said Luscious.

"Caaaaw," said the crow, pecking at his leg.

"Help!" Luscious called. "Get him off me!" He made himself into a ball. "Get him off me!"

B. J. pulled his slingshot out of his back pocket and the unused skipping stone out of his front pocket. He closed one eye, aimed for the crow's head and shot, just as the door to the icehouse opened. Luscious and the crow came tumbling off the roof and landed in a heap.

"Owww," moaned Luscious.

"You killed Jim," said a light-skinned black man wearing yellow suspenders, a wifebeater and a mustache. He looked to be about fifty.

"That's your bird?" asked B. J.

"That was my bird. Looks like you clipped him in the head."

"I'm sorry, Mister. Really sorry."

"Owww, my *shoulder*."

"You called him Jim?" B. J. asked.

"Yes. That was Jim Crow."

"If I hadda known he belonged to you I wouldna shot him. It's just, he was beating on my uncle."

"Your uncle was spying. And trespassing."

"I just wanted to see who was inside," said Luscious, rubbing his shoulder.

The man went over and stood above Luscious with his fists on his hips. His shadow fell over the boy. "Me," he said. "That's who. Now that you know, you can bury Jim."

"With what?" asked Luscious.

"Your bare hands will do. Start digging."

Luscious started digging.

"Where do you two live?"

"We stay at the end of Saw Log Lane," said B. J.

Slowly, the man grinned. "In a pink shotgun shack?"

Luscious looked up with wide eyes.

"Yeah. How'd you know that?" B. J. asked.

The man turned around and walked back into the icehouse. "When you're done with Jim, come inside," he called. "I'm not finished with you."

The boys plucked and pocketed two of Jim's tail feathers. Then they took their sweet time burying him.

"What do you think he's gonna do to us?" whispered Luscious.

"Can't say."

"I don't think we should go in."

"He knows where we live."

"You shouldna told him."

"We better just go get what we got coming."

They stepped down into the icehouse. The man was up on a stool, brandishing a saw.

"Sweet Jesus," said Luscious.

The man looked up at the hole in the ceiling. "This is going to make a fine skylight when I'm through," he said.

B. J. was surprised at how cramped it was inside. In his mind, the icehouse had always been deep, like a cave, but this looked more like a little barn.

"One of you can take that broom there and sweep up. The other can start opening those." He pointed at the wooden crates that were lined up against the wall opposite the door. Then he started ripping at the ceiling. Luscious went for the broom. B. J. walked up to one of the bigger crates. He pried off its side and was flooded in an avalanche of newspaper confetti. A face looked down at him.

"It's a stone lady," he gasped.

"It's a sculpture," laughed the man. "That's what I do."

The next day they went into town to look at the guitar Luscious was saving to buy from the pawnshop with his shampoo money. Dudley, the waterhead man, was polishing the knickknacks. His face was badly scarred.

"Ain't she fine?" said Luscious. The guitar had no strings but was so shiny you could see your face in it. There was a five-dollar price tag around its neck.

"Don't be putting your grubby fingers on that guitar, boy," said the junkman behind the counter. He was chewing on a toothpick.

"I'm saving to buy it."

"Git out and come back when you got the money."

Dudley dropped a china figurine. It was a bride, and she broke in half at the waist when she hit the floor. "Uh-oh, uh-oh," said Dudley, holding his head.

"That's it, Frankeniggerstein," said the junkman, "you can forget about getting paid this week."

They passed by Miss Mary's house on the way back. She was out on her front porch reading the newspaper.

"Hey, Miss Mary," called the boys at the same time.

"Hey, boys." She waved. "You getting ready to go up to New Orleans, B. J.?"

"Yes, ma'am."

"Never thought I'd see the day. We're all so proud of you, son."

At home, Nan and the man from the icehouse were sitting in the front room with plates of German chocolate cake balanced on their laps.

"There they are!" said Nan.

"We just wanted to see who was inside!" said Luscious.

"We didn't mean any harm," added B. J.

"What are you going on about?" asked Nan. "I'd like you to meet Roland Favré. This is Luscious and Bernard Jr., B. J. for short."

"Pleased to meet you," said the man from the icehouse.

"Mr. Favré's been in Europe. He used to stay under my roof long time ago. Now he's a world-famous artist."

"I wouldn't say that."

"That's why I did. I don't raise duds."

"Pleased to meet you," said Luscious and B. J. at the same time.

"Are you on Nan's wall?" asked B. J.

"I'm the one in the sailor suit," said Roland Favré.

"Bernard Jr. here reminds me of you when you were small, Roland. He goes through books like nobody's business. Matter fact, he just won himself a scholarship to a fancy boys' school up in New Orleans. He's gon' be a professor."

"Is that so."

"Yessir," said B. J.

"He's the first colored boy they ever admitted."

"You must be very proud, Zanobia."

"I'm saving to buy a guitar," said Luscious.

On the first Saturday in August, while Luscious was helping Miss Pauline at the beauty parlor, B. J. sat on a stool in the center of the old icehouse rereading another library book while Roland sculpted his head.

The icehouse had transformed. Roland Favré had cleared away the weeds and installed two windows in each wall, in addition to the one in the ceiling. The place was flooded with light.

"Hold your chin up a little more."

"Is that Gabriel?" asked B. J., referring to a bronze bust with three-foot wings.

"No. That's just a regular angel without a name."

"Oh. I guess he's my favorite out of all of them." His eyes scanned the studio and stopped on the plaster head of a man with a rope around his neck. "Who's that one?" he asked. The face was contorted in pain.

"That's the angel's head."

"But—they don't look like they go together."

"All my sculptures go together. They're all different parts of the same being. Yours will be part of it too, when I'm done."

B. J. thought about that for a little while. Then he asked, "Are you a communist?"

Roland grinned. "Who told you that?"

"My uncle said they were talking about you at the Curly-Q. They were calling you a Red."

"That's probably the only piece of gossip those old hens had right."

"You mean you are a communist?"

"Yes, I'm a communist. Hold still."

B. J. held still for a long time. His butt started to go numb. A freight train rolled by, shaking the studio with the tail of its wind. "Mr. Favré?"

"Yes, son."

"Why'd you move back here?"

"I missed home. Try to keep your head steady. I thought I'd come back for a spell when I heard this place was for sale."

"My father used to work here when it was a icehouse. He was a baseball player too."

"Is that right?"

"He was going to play for the Birmingham Black Barons."

"Hold still."

"I hate it here. When I leave, I'm never coming back."

"That's how I used to feel." Roland dipped his right hand in a bucket of water at his feet and smoothed his palm over the ball of clay. "You know what I missed when I was gone?"

"What?"

"The way the bay smells. And the Spanish moss in the trees. Turn clockwise. That's good. Stay like that. Hold your chin up." He started shaving off the excess clay with his knife. "This place is beautiful and ugly at the same time. Just like a human being."

A slight woman in a droopy yellow hat stood on the front porch holding her son's hand. He was so skinny his wrist bones were poking out. Nan answered the door.

"Sorry to bother you," said the woman.

"You're not bothering me, Ophelia," said Nan. "I'm happy to see you. It's been a while. My, my, is this your little boy?"

"Yes."

Nan put her hands on her knees and bent down. "He sure has grown, hasn't he?"

"Say hello to Ms. Zanobia, Willie."

"H-h-h-hey," said Willie. His two front teeth were missing.

"Would you two like to come in?"

"No, thank you. We can't stay; we just come by to ask—I'm heading to Detroit next month to see about a job, and I heard one of your boys was moving out."

"I see."

"So I was wondering if Willie here could stay with you for a while."

"Of course," Nan said. She put her hand on the boy's head and tilted it back slightly, so he was looking up at her. "Of course he can."

"Just 'til I get settled up there and can save up enough to send for him."

"Ain't That a Shame," was playing full volume on the radio. B. J. was watching Luscious dance with Nan in the lamplight of the kitchen. The shutters were open to let in the night air. "Shake your hips, Nan!" shouted Luscious. "Pretend you're wearing a red satin dress!" He twirled her around and dipped her.

"Let me go, chile, I can't breathe," she laughed.

Luscious picked up his brand-new secondhand guitar and started playing along with the song. B. J. put his head down on the table and started to cry. He was leaving in three days.

"Bernard Jr.?" Nan came over and put her hand on his back. "Shut that off, Luscious. What is it? What's troubling you, brown sugar?"

B. J. just sobbed.

"Luscious, bring your nephew another piece of pecan pie."

"I don't want it," B. J. choked.

"Good Lord, something must be truly the matter. Come on; let's go sit on the porch. You can tell me all about it and I can smoke my pipe. Luscious, cut that noise and finish the dishes."

B. J. slumped down on the steps. Nan eased into her rocking chair. "I think that fool broke my back." She started filling her pipe with tobacco. The cicadas were buzzing a blanket of sound over them. A sphinx moth hovered in the gypsum weed growing by the steps. Beyond that it was blackness. There was no moon, and you couldn't see as far as the pecan tree. B. J.'s eyes stung. He removed his glasses and rubbed his eyes. Nan held a match to the bowl of her pipe and drew in several quick little kisses to light the tobacco. They sat like that for a long time.

"Out of all the children I've raised, your daddy was the cockiest," she said. "Used to roll up his sleeves and strut around here like a peacock. He was pretty, and he knew it. Sort of like your Uncle Luscious," she laughed. "All the girls was sweet on him, and he broke every one of their hearts when he married your mama. But they was a perfect match. You couldn't find a better-looking pair than them two."

Nan exhaled a series of smoke rings. They dilated and dissolved, one after the other. "The only thing he loved more than your mama was baseball. You heard about that I guess."

B. J. nodded his head.

"When your daddy was six or seven he asked me for a baseball bat. I got him one for Christmas—he must have been six 'cause he couldn't read yet. We come out back here so I could throw him some pitches. Let me tell you, that bat was bigger than he was, so I pitched the ball real slow. Underhand. He swung at it and he missed and he got this real mad look on his face. So I pitched to him again and the same thing happened again. I threw the ball for him twenty times and he missed twenty times. Then he said, 'Throw it like they do for real.' So I pitched overhand to him and he whacked that ball so hard it broke the window behind you."

B. J. turned his head and looked at the window. He could see Luscious in there, scrubbing the supper dishes.

Nan's voice slowed down. "Some people was jealous of your daddy. It looked like he was gonna make a success of himself, and they called him uppity. He wasn't uppity; he was headstrong and proud. But they didn't see it like that. So they made a example of him."

B. J. started shimmying his leg on the porch step. "What they do to him?"

"A bunch of them got liquored up and ambushed him over at the icehouse one night. He used to work a midnight shift and then cart the ice around, starting when the sun came up. Sleep in the morning. Wake up in the afternoon."

"What they do to him?"

"They kilt him."

"How?"

Nan lowered her pipe, then raised it again and took a puff. "They lit him on fire."

B. J.'s leg stopped shimmying. He sat very still.

"Next afternoon Sarah came over here all upset. They were renting a little place on Hickama Street at the time, and they were getting ready to leave for Birmingham after you was born. It wasn't nothing but a fixed-up lean-to really, but Sarah made it cozy in there. She came over here and told me Bernard never came home and she had a bad feeling. So we went knocking on doors, asking folks if he delivered their ice that morning, and they all said no.

"We went by the icehouse and asked Dollar Hemply if he knew anything. Dollar said when he come to work, the door was wide open, and some of the ice was melting where the sunshine was coming in. When he said that I felt real cold, and I knew something was wrong."

Indoors, Luscious started plucking his new guitar. The notes flew out at them like bats.

"The last place I could think to look was the baseball field. I told Sarah he probably went over there to practice some with some friends. I was trying to calm her down. Dollar rode us over there in the cart and what we saw—it looked like someone had a bonfire in the middle of the baseball diamond, right where the pitcher's mound was, and it was still smoking."

Nan cleared her throat.

"Then we saw Bernard—what was left—hanging up in a oak tree over to the side of the field. Sarah said it wasn't him, but I knew it was. I just knew. After the funeral she went back with an ax to chop down that tree. Broke her water trying. That's how you come into the world."

B. J. didn't know what to say, so he didn't say anything. He hugged his shoulders with his arms and looked between his knees. He felt seasick, and his mouth was dry.

"Hate works like a circle if you don't stop it somewhere. I didn't tell you all this before now 'cause I didn't want you hating God and hating them. If you thought that—if you came up hating them 'cause of what they did, you couldn't come so far. But look at you. Look how you been blessed by God. I'm *so* proud of you."

Out in the blackness a screech owl cried. The porch seemed to tilt then. B. J. stretched his neck out like a turtle and vomited over the steps.

"I don't wanna go," said Luscious. It was raining. He was up in the pecan tree, and all you could see were his legs. Nan was standing below him in her lavender dress, holding an umbrella. B. J. and his suitcase were waiting out front in Roland Favré's truck.

"What you mean you don't wanna go?"

"I'm staying."

"Don't make me climb that tree, Luscious."

"I don't have to go if I don't feel like it. You can't make me."

"You get your monkey tail down here right now."

"No."

"You gon' make him miss his train."

"I don't care. It ain't like we brothers."

"If you don't come down this second—"

"Noooooo!" yelled Luscious. The word cracked in the middle.

Two minutes later Nan slid into the cab of Roland's truck and shut the door.

"Your uncle can't bear to see you go, honey," she told B. J. "He wanted me to give you this." She handed him a cigar box that said "Loshis" on it. The windshield wiper was swinging back and forth, making a hush-swish sound. "Better step on it, Roland. That train won't wait for us."

B. J. turned his head and watched the pink shack getting smaller through a wash of rain.

When they pulled up to the depot, everyone was there to see him off, close to a hundred of them, gathered under a forest of black umbrellas. B. J.'s glasses had fogged up. He couldn't see all of their faces, but he recognized King Benoit and Ms. Mary and Father Jacques at the front of the crowd. Gracie Champlain was there too, with her whole family, and there was Dudley, without an umbrella, getting sopping wet.

"You gotta hurry, honey, they're boarding already," said Nan, and before he knew it he was rushing by them, and Roland was squeezing his shoulder and wishing him luck, and Nan was telling him to be careful, and they were pushing him up, and the doors closed behind him and he had to find a seat.

"Two cars back, nigger!" a man barked.

The train began to roll, and he could see them through the window, one big black mass raising up its hands. They didn't know what he would find when he got there.

Emily Raboteau holds an MFA in Creative Writing from New York University. She is the recipient of both the 2001 Nelson Algren Award for Short Fiction and a Pushcart Prize. Her stories have appeared or will appear in the *Chicago Tribune*, *Tin House*, *African Voices*, *Callaloo*, *Transition* and *Best American Short Stories 2003*. "Bernard Jr.'s Uncle Luscious" is part of her novel-in-stories which Henry Holt will publish next year.

Reviews

The Body of Water
by Walter Bargen
Illustrated by Michael Sleadd
Timberline Press, 2003, 123 pp., $20
(paper)

Three chapbooks, originally published from 1990 to 1999, are brought together as a trilogy in this handsome volume that provides a rich sample of Bargen's work. Walter Bargen's poetic world is often dark and threatening, sometimes despairing, but the poetry itself provides the lifeline that saves the reader from drowning.

The first part, *Yet Other Waters*, begins: "This is drought," and continues with recurrent images of diminished or disappearing flow, of the longing for water and for experience, for immersion in life itself, which is, however, uncertain and dangerous. The persistent images of fundamental elements—water, air, heat and cold—remind us of the uncertainties of life in the natural world. Humans are part of nature but imagine they can create certainties, continuities, stabilities. Bargen's human dramas remind us of the transience of our fantasies of permanence.

The middle section, *The Vertical River*, echoes a great tradition of lyric poetry as it confronts the uneasy encounters between human consciousness and the physical universe. Poems like "Into the Storm" and "The New Francis" may remind us of Shelley and Wallace Stevens, sometimes Keats or Richard Wilbur, but never as imitation or borrowing—more as the work of a kindred spirit newly experiencing the power of the storm or the sudden awareness of the otherness of natural things. The title phrase of this volume comes from a brilliant poem, "Newton Revisited," describing a rock climber who succeeds in his perilous ascent just as a ferocious storm hits, creating doubt that he can survive as the rock face is transformed into a "vertical river." Somehow, "as if what he was descending was/water," he survives and steps "on grounded principles." But such grounding is a matter of hope in Bargen's world, where "I want to believe/. . . that the world/will not harm me or anyone else."

Recurring images (of frogs, of mirrors and glass—broken or impervious and destructive, of birds and litter) link the third section, *Water Breathing Air*, to the earlier volumes, but the mood has darkened; the language is more public and epigrammatic, the poems more clearly focused on the damage done by the human presence on earth. From the wanton killing of turtles that don't know they can't safely cross a road to the ominously declining populations of frogs to the depressing spectacle, in "The Croak of Obsession," of treasures accumulated only to be discarded at flea markets, these poems variously indict our behavior.

Bargen's poetry is intellectually complex, rich in imagery and word-play (though sometimes the clever-ness seems a digression from the pure power of the imagery), emotionally engaging as it evokes the everyday encounters that sometimes help us to feel sheltered but more often remind us of fragility and transience. "If you wait, you grow old, nothing/more. Traveling light is your only/illu-minating illusion," Bargen writes in "Map to the Party," a rethinking of the climber's encounter with the storm that achieves a more complex understanding of the necessity of going on. Whether for the pure poetic pleasure of Bargen's expert manipu-lations of language and poetic tradi-tion, or for the emotional power of his sympathetic encounters with the world, *The Body of Water* is one vol-ume of poetry to be read and reread with pleasure and with the pain that accompanies deeper understanding. (TD)

A Short History of Nearly Everything
by Bill Bryson
Broadway Books, 2003, 560 pp., $27.50

The photographs taken by NASA of the earth floating in the blackness of space are among the most arrest-ing images of the last fifty years. Those taken from the distance of the moon show the earth as a surprisingly small orb wrapped in a thin, blue, cloud-swirled atmosphere. Like so much else that we have been learning in the last few decades, the image of spaceship earth—this delicate, cell-like vessel—suggests the interdepen-dency of life, a subject too long neglected.

Most of us are aware that humans are destructive. The full record of our recklessness will never be known, although it is increasingly evident that for thousands of years we have been wiping out other species on a weekly basis, often for no apparent reason. In the 18th and 19th centu-ries, the majority of "new" species of birds or turtles or lizards encoun-tered on islands or island chains were exterminated within a few years. Pre-historic humans and native tribes, with some exceptions, were no dif-ferent from modern man in this ten-dency, although the increased human population and destructive activity over the last couple of hundred years have considerably enhanced our abil-ity to scorch the earth.

No one really knows how likely human behavior is to make the earth uninhabitable, but scientists now generally agree that earthwide catas-trophes can happen shockingly fast, due to unstoppable chains of events. Much of what we do is by ignorance, and our ignorance—for example, regarding the effects we are having on weather-changing ocean life and on the atmosphere—is vast. One would hope that once we know defin-itively that we are wrecking either the atmosphere or the ocean, we could stop doing it and try to remedy the problem. The truth is that once the "for-sure" light is blinking, it will probably be too late. Global disasters can and have happened repeatedly in earth's history. Paleoanthropolo-gists studying human DNA believe that the people currently living on the earth came from a remarkably small population, probably because at some point in the past everybody else was wiped out.

These are among the more sobering issues that Bill Bryson discusses in *A Short History of Nearly Everything*, a book with something of a dual personality. It begins as a cheerful miscellany of the history of science, starting with the ancients and touching on major figures and fields during succeeding centuries. The author approaches his subjects through the personalities of the scientists. Occasionally, he seems overly concerned to demonstrate, as if to a roomful of bored high school students, that all these people were really *weird* and *interesting*. Still, it is amusing to read about such characters as the paranoid genius Isaac Newton, author of the *Principia*, the most important document in the history of science. Newton was known to do such things as get halfway out of bed and forget to actually stand up. He figured out the basic laws of physics with apparently little effort, then spent most of his time fruitlessly puzzling over how to turn heavy metals into gold.

The author also depicts many of the lesser-known characters from science, such as the Swede Karl Scheele, who was smart enough to discover eight elements but at the same time dumb enough to taste everything he discovered or had in his lab, including hydrocyanic acid. He was found at forty-three with a stunned look on his face, dead, surrounded by an array of items, any of which could have killed him. From the 19th century we hear about Dr. Gideon Mantell, dinosaur discoverer, and his nemesis, the odious Richard Owen, the only man the gentle Darwin was said to hate. Owen tried to gain credit for the discovery of dinosaurs by taking advantage of Mantell's weakened state after he fell from his carriage and was dragged through the streets in London—an accident that left him a near invalid. When the poor doctor died, Owen took his broken spine as one of the biological curiosities in the museum that he established, London's Natural History Museum.

Bryson focuses on the most visible scientific fields through the centuries. For example, he describes important figures in elementary chemistry in the 18th century; geology and paleontology in the 19th; and astronomy, biology, tectonics and atomic science in the 20th. The book's split personality becomes obvious in these later chapters, about subjects that at times plunge the author into gloom.

Still, this is a rewarding book, especially for the reader who enjoys "facts" and history—with some thoroughly entertaining gossip mixed in. (SM)

The Life You Save May Be Your Own: An American Pilgrimage by Paul Elie
FSG, 2003, 554 pp., $27

How does one write about a literary movement that never really was? In Paul Elie's *The Life You Save May Be Your Own*, the answer seems to be: find four contemporary writers with a shared faith, describe their lives in clear, simple prose and let their stories offer whatever connections may arise. It's a risky strategy, especially when three of the four writers—Thomas Merton,

Flannery O'Connor and Walker Percy—spent their lives in near seclusion and, with the exception of a brief visit between Merton and Percy, never met. The fourth, Dorothy Day, founded the Catholic Worker movement and devoted much of her literary life to publishing a political newspaper and doing social work. By these tokens, Elie's project should be a disaster.

The threat of ruin that hangs over the opening pages quickly dissipates, though, as Elie introduces the four writers in terms of a shared pilgrimage, a thematic link that neatly serves the rest of the book: "Already, they saw themselves as representative figures whose concerns were characteristically modern; and already, they were sharpening their skills as writers—trying to describe religious experience, to imagine it, to convey it to the reader as believable, exciting, profound," he writes.

Merton's pilgrimage, famously described in his autobiography *The Seven Storey Mountain*, began in his twenties, when he converted to Catholicism, eventually becoming a Trappist monk. The irony of "celebrity" that would attend his solitary life is nicely dramatized by Elie, who contrasts Merton's inward journey with Dorothy Day's outward role as activist, publisher and political writer. A correspondence between the two (Merton published several essays in Day's newspaper) reveals a sense of community that transcends a religious creed and throws a larger light on the solitary acts of writing and thinking and—to borrow a phrase from O'Connor—the habit of being. The two discuss their opposition to the Vietnam War, as well as the novels of Walker Percy. They disagree about the desirable scope of nonviolent activism, then close their letters with requests for prayers for the sick and dying. Merton's life would end, tragically, during a trip to Asia; the *Catholic Worker* would survive Dorothy Day, whose offices Elie visits in the epilogue. In observing, with a novelist's eye, the "beat-up chairs and a cast-iron stove out of a Grimm tale" where "a pot of coffee brews perpetually," Elie gives us an elegant mix of elegy and hopefulness that informs much of the book.

Flannery O'Connor and Walker Percy were pilgrims of a different sort. Both were Southerners, Catholic, writers of novels, short stories and essays; both chose to live isolated lives in small towns. And both, through Elie's assured prose, emerge as artists with an equal concern for articulating their ideas of faith as well as rendering "the highest possible justice to the visible universe." O'Connor, best known for her short stories, struggled with the novel form. Percy's first novel, *The Moviegoer*, won the National Book Award in 1962, although Percy was never again to match its artfulness. Percy's essays, often political, are closest perhaps to Merton's, who, Elie tells us, greeted Percy's visit at the monastery wearing jeans and a T-shirt, offering a glass of bourbon.

Merton read Percy; Percy read Merton; O'Connor read Merton; Day read Percy—Elie connects the dots, and a picture emerges. Watching it slowly develop is one of the first pleasures of reading Elie's book. But a secondary reward, perhaps even more enjoyable, is the fun of all the minor figures who flit in and out of view, creating a world that feels as densely populated and interconnected as a Dickens novel. Robert Lowell, Joan Baez, the Dalai Lama, Czeslaw Milosz, Robert Giroux, Shelby Foote, John Kennedy Toole, D. T. Suzuki, and Pope John Paul II, all make appearances here. It is, Elie suggests, a literary movement that extends beyond the scope of these four writers.

If there are any limitations to Elie's book, one might be that the somewhat democratic process of dividing the chapters into equal sections for each writer doesn't always satisfy. At times Merton, the most prolific of the group, nearly overwhelms the book. Still, *The Life You Save May Be Your Own* is successful—intelligently written, with all the visual grace and sensibility of a good novel. In attempting to render a literary movement built upon the mysteries of faith, Elie has written an important book that reads like an ordinary one, plainly stated, with a shimmer of greatness. (AV)

The Teammates: A Portrait of a Friendship
by David Halberstam
Hyperion, 2003, 217 pp., $22.95

The Teammates, David Halberstam's newest book on American sports, is an account of four Boston Red Sox teammates: Dom DiMaggio, Bobby Doerr, Johnny Pesky and Ted Williams. The four came to the major leagues together and anchored the talented Red Sox teams of the 1940s, when baseball was America's true pastime, the pitching mound was five inches higher and St. Louis was

the westernmost *and* southernmost city to have a major league team. Halberstam's book was inspired by a trip Pesky and DiMaggio made in October 2001 to visit Williams, ill and homebound in Florida (because he was caring for his sick wife, Doerr was unable to make the trip). *The Teammates* recounts the early lives of the four players, the evolution of their friendships, their successful, though heartbreaking, careers in Red Sox uniforms, and their transitions into life after baseball.

The Florida pilgrimage may have been the springboard for Halberstam's book, but precious little narrative is dedicated to the trip, made by car from Boston. Only one chapter—ten pages—is given to depicting the reunion, which is described in an understated and poignant manner.

The book's subtitle, "A Portrait of a Friendship," might lead readers to expect a profound exploration of the nature of friendship. At the least, one might anticipate an account of the strong bonds among four teammates. But the friendships will strike most readers as pretty mundane. In fact, we seldom see all four friends together.

Halberstam is most successful in weaving the stories of the Red Sox teammates into the fabric of midcentury American life. *The Teammates* is about baseball, but it provides snapshots into the lives of immigrant families—Pesky is the son of Croatians; DiMaggio, Italians. It shows talented baseball players willing to pause in their athletic careers to serve their country during World War II and the Korean conflict. Playing in an era when team owners controlled the game and athlete salaries were in the tens of thousands—Pesky's highest salary was $22,500—the four Red Sox players provide a sharp contrast to today's cocky athlete millionaires. In the 1940s, major league players often maintained other jobs in the off-season, and it was rare that a player left baseball for full-blown retirement. Pesky, a player-turned-coach-and-Boston-broadcaster, and DiMaggio, who founded and ran a successful upholstery manufacturing company, were typical in their after-baseball careers.

Told in crisp prose without sports jargon and enlivened by generous quotations from the subjects, the narrative offers an insider's view of four men and their successful runs in the major leagues. For Pesky and DiMaggio (the younger brother of Yankee Hall of Famer Joe DiMaggio), success came despite long odds. Pesky was small—5'9", 168 pounds—and DiMaggio was plagued by poor eyesight.

Halberstam provides plenty of interesting nuggets for baseball junkies, from stories about spit-ball hurlers to theories on hitting advanced by Williams, the last player to bat .400. We learn that years after sending Babe Ruth to the rival Yankees, the Red Sox passed on an opportunity to sign a young Willie Mays. Halberstam's narrative of the 1946 World Series (which the Sox lost in seven games to the Cardinals) is riveting. The author presents an in-depth analysis of the dramatic seventh game and the key plays that led to the heartbreaking defeat for a franchise that last won the championship in 1918. In a startling revelation, Halberstam's book exonerates Pesky, who has long been blamed for the seventh-game loss because of his inexplicable delay in making a relay throw as Enos Slaughter sprinted home from first base with the deciding run.

What is most notable about *The Teammates* is its clear-eyed portrait of Williams, the dominant friend, the one who seems to have united the four teammates. A twice-decorated war veteran known for his sweet batting stroke, the complex Williams is portrayed in a balanced way: one moment he is the consummate professional and the loyal friend who shares his wealth with less fortunate teammates; the next he is thin-skinned, with a mercurial temper, often prickly with reporters and fans. Always he is a perfectionist, inclined to debating his opinions, whether about baseball, fishing or the proper way to slice a grapefruit. As Halberstam jokes: Joe DiMaggio may have hit in 56 consecutive games, but Williams "won 33,277 consecutive arguments." (BG)

Kingdom of the Instant
by Rodney Jones
Mariner Books, 2004, 112 pp., $22

Kingdom of the Instant is Rodney Jones's seventh volume of poetry. His previous book, *Elegy for the Southern Drawl*, was a Pulitzer finalist. Among admirers of Jones's earlier work, that book surely elicited more lamentations for its author than praise for its poetry. *Elegy* did seem to be saying good-bye, and hence turning away from, a certain landscape that Jones had mined with much success before. All too often the poetry in *Elegy* seem dried out, sad and, well . . . academic.

It is a pleasure to announce that Rodney Jones has regained his equilibrium and produced a collection of poetry that line by line, poem by poem, has one of the highest percentages of flesh-and-bloodness to be found in contemporary poetry. "Keeping Time," the exquisitely crafted first poem, contains the proscription, "no/more leaden introspection, have foot." *Kingdom of the Instant* turns that proscription into a promise and mostly keeps it. Which is not at all to say that Jones isn't introspective; but in this book he gets the lead out.

Rodney Jones's strength has always been the South, though he is no mere regional writer. He seems to have made peace with this fact in "Backward," the poem from which the collection's title is taken. Alluding to his earlier poems, Jones admits, "I'm stickered and plaster-patched with the past,/with fencerows, moo-cows, and fields' dark mire,/with bog wallows, pussy jokes, and sermon fire./ One ridge I lived."

Jones has been able to mine that one ridge, to turn it over and over in his mind and present it to his audience in such a way that its facets reflect life to us. He is older now, successful if not famous. Now that he is finally comfortable with this place, and with his perspective, the insights return. The regained equilibrium is exemplified by "Strip," reminiscent of "Tintern Abbey," the first section of "Five Walks for the Nineteenth Century." After dropping off the car, while walking to the college, Jones steps off the pavement into memory and inspiration, as the Illinois mud transports him to Alabama: "the sucky mush, swamp gas, and beavered willows/where I would go in foggy adolescence . . . . And now came the small trance

where poems/start up from the wet shoetops" but only "to get short-circuited/by a startling Camaro full of vagrant redneck kids." The poem is peopled with Snoop Doggy Dogg, Colonel Sanders and, yes, Wordsworth and his sister.

Then there's "A Whisper Fight at the Peck Funeral Home," a poem more wondrously elegiac than anything to be found in *Elegy*. The poem is partly storytelling, partly meditative, morbidly comical, often tragic and always powerful. It is a long poem, and it's easy to forget along the way that it started with one particular corpse, whose identity was initially unknown to the reader. But when the "cold eulogy" appears, and Jones obliquely communicates the deceased's identity, we find the explanation for the poet's new comfort, his new perspective, in the revelation that the dead man was his father: "I still eat at his table. For years I wore his shoes." (SS)

Things My Mother Never Told Me by Blake Morrison
Granta, 2003, 338 pp., $24.95

Things My Mother Never Told Me follows Morrison's initial foray into memoir, the successful *And When Did You Last See Your Father?* (1995). Whereas *Father* was written on the heels of the death of Morrison's father, Arthur, *Mother* focuses on the recently deceased Agnes.

On the surface the premise has potential. Agnes Morrison has all the makings of a viable lead: she was a female doctor when they were rarer, an Irish expatriate itinerant in England, a woman with enough religious and romantic confusion to imbue her with depth. A compelling figure, but Agnes is almost pathological in her secrecy. As a result, the memoir takes on the feeling of a detective novel, with Blake Morrison sleuthing out his mother's carefully concealed past.

Morrison has an important weapon in this struggle: letters preserved by his father. These are lovely exchanges between Arthur and Agnes over the span of their courtship, most written while Arthur was doctoring in various theaters of World War II and Agnes was doctoring back home. These letters are the true gems of the book, lively and human. We come to understand Arthur, to cheer for him. And yet, despite being privy to thousands of Agnes's words, often truly heartfelt and naked, we never quite grasp her in the same way.

Perhaps Agnes's contradictions are what make her so hard to assess. Subordinate in marriage, she is nonetheless the more capable of the two family physicians. Shy and withdrawn, she intrigues a wartime poet enough that he dedicates one of his collections to her. Even her name suggests obliqueness. She takes on a number of different names, finally settling on Kim at the request of her husband. This passivity extends throughout her life, to the detriment of the memoir, for while the idea of a wife who accepts a new name out of love for her husband is intriguing, the question of why a husband would want to rechristen a wife is more so. Arthur is so charismatic that in Morrison's book he often upstages his wife. This is not necessarily a problem for the reader, who has no vested interest

in either character, but Morrison forces the issue, driving his father into the background and teasing his mother forward through commentary and intrusive narration. Author and reader alike are frustrated as, again and again, Agnes (or Gennie, or Kim)'s ethereal essence evades her son's attempts to capture it. He never manages to pin her down, and the memoir suffers as a result.

As Morrison points out, this story has certain inherent hindrances: it is the tale of a courtship, without the suspense of wondering how it will end. And the letters between Arthur and Agnes, whose energy fuels the memoir, end once the lovers are united. Once they share a bed, they no longer direct their emotions to paper. There is a satisfying conclusion to *Father:* Arthur Morrison dies suddenly and mysteriously. Agnes Morrison, on the other hand, succumbs to old age, a degeneration that mirrors the finale of this book. Hers is the quiet end that we all hope to have in life but that does not fit literary protagonists nearly so well. (MP)

The Conversations: Walter Murch and the Art of Editing Film by Michael Ondaatje
Alfred A. Knopf, 2002, 368 pp., $35

To read Michael Ondaatje's *The Conversations: Walter Murch and the Art of Editing Film* is to eavesdrop on two artists of almost boundless powers discussing their respective creative passions. *The Conversations* is a series of five entertaining and illuminating dialogues between Ondaatje, author of *The English Patient,* and Walter Murch, film editor of the movie. In this fascinating peek into a cinematic craft, Ondaatje reveals the genie behind the Hollywood curtain.

Inasmuch as movies create a collective cultural memory, Murch's art has imprinted the American psyche: he has had a hand in such iconic films as *The Godfather, American Graffiti, The Conversation, The Godfather, Part II, Apocalypse Now, Ghost* and *The Talented Mr. Ripley*. Murch was the artist who flipped the switches, layered the sound and moved the images to make moviegoers believe that walls really do bend to the contours of ghosts and that there really are men walking among us who love the smell of napalm in the morning.

With the utmost sensitivity, he must weave the raw elements of film the footage, the sound, the dialogue, the music into a coherent whole. In his own words: "It's really a question of orchestration: organizing the images and sounds in a way that is interesting, and digestible by the audience. One of your obligations as an editor is to drench yourself in the sensibility of the film, to the point where you're live to the smallest details and also the most important themes."

Ondaatje's appreciation for the subtlety of Murch's craft is evident throughout these wide-ranging discussions, which cover such topics as the relation of film to dreams and the seiche tone of San Francisco Bay. With its easy style and question-and-answer format, *Conversations* is a book for readers who appreciate good dialogue and for moviegoers who want to understand what a film editor does. Interspersed throughout are photographs of movie outtakes

as well as essays by George Lucas and Francis Ford Coppola that testify to the esteem in which these two titans hold Murch.

It was his friendship with Lucas and Coppola that launched Murch's career. By the mid-'60s, the old Hollywood system was collapsing and new filmmakers were expressing their creative visions. Murch became friends with fellow USC student George Lucas, who knew Francis Ford Coppola. Eventually Lucas and Coppola hired Murch to create the sound montage and rerecording mixer for one of their early films, *The Rain People*.

For Murch, it was a chance to rediscover a childhood love. As an eleven-year-old, he would record the street sounds rising to his parents' Riverside Drive apartment in Manhattan. He tells Ondaatje, "And then I discovered the concept of physically editing tape—that you could rearrange it by cutting out sections and putting those sections in a different order."

For Murch, sound is not only a means of creating atmosphere but a way of shifting perspective: dialogue is the moon, he tells Ondaatje; sound, the stars. By manipulating it, an editor can increase or lessen a character's preoccupation or his self-awareness and give the audience clues to what's happening off screen, clues the character may not be aware of.

The desert in *The English Patient* was a special challenge. Murch's task was nothing less than creating the sound of silence. It was doubly difficult because the particular tone of the desert's silence doesn't match the emotion its vast, empty space evokes.

To create an aural counterpart of that emotion, Murch interwove a series of insect-like clicks with the tiny abrasive sound of sand particles rubbing against each other. In effect, he created a sound that wasn't there to match the emotional tenor of a scene that was itself fiction.

In the visual dimension, Murch culls raw footage to obtain the precise frame, revealing a deeper, more complex meaning than either the writer, the actor or the director may have expected. To film the average movie requires twenty-five times the film that is in the final cut. In *Apocalypse Now* the ratio was a hundred to one. At some point, perhaps on the third take, perhaps on the thirty-third, an actor will blink or inadvertently twist his mouth a certain way when he says how much he loved his father. Murch will seize that second, giving the audience to understand what the character cannot admit to himself: that in the deepest chamber of his heart, he feels his father was a narcissistic nincompoop.

In these dialogues—and they really are two-way discussions—novelist and filmmaker share the understanding that the creative process is completed only when a viewer or reader layers the narrative with his own sensibilities. That critical synapse between the objective story and what the viewer or reader apprehends is the third dimension where magic happens.

Given the wide range of topics this book covers, its biggest weakness is its organization. Like all conversations, especially those between dynamic individuals, these carom from topic to topic, and some subjects, like *The English Patient*, come up again and

again. While Ondaatje does supply subheads throughout the chapters, their titles are not especially helpful. "Ka-lunk" and "Wideo" aren't useful to a reader who wants to reread a critical point, and unfortunately the page numbers of the subheads aren't on the contents page.

These problems aside, *The Conversations* gives unique insight into a craft that has made us all sit and laugh, cry, cheer and gasp together with a group of strangers in a pitch-black room. Michael Ondaatje lifts the curtain and shows us that movie magic isn't wizardry at all but a perfect blend of consummate skill and creative instinct. (PS)

The Standing Wave
by Gabriel Spera
Perennial, 2003, 96 pp., $12.95

Like the aerialist in the poem of the same title, one of the strongest in this collection, Gabriel Spera tiptoes a fine line, maintaining a balance between formalism and free verse, traditional tropes and verbal originality. When Spera casts his long, clause-riddled sentences into a formal structure, the result is often spectacular. The sentences tumble down through the stanzas like downhill skiers, swerving almost breathtakingly to clip the gate of each rhyme: "And he would be lured, surely, by the trucks/plowing like mollusks/down the glistening freeways, the half-crown/of islands that pacify the harbor, where yawls/anchored off the yacht club docks, like minnows/browsing, nose/the coming currents with their sleek bright hulls/all schooled and aligned."

Spera is constantly complicating his images, adding metaphor upon metaphor, as in this description of olive picking: "My hand's small tongues grow blacker/in swallowing the dark fruit/dangling like gems of tar or/opulent mussels clustered/to some sea beast's restless/green and silvered mane." The result is a desire to crawl back through the poems and start to unpack them, even as the verbal energy thrusts us forward.

These poems do not rely on form alone for their power. Spera, whose book was selected by Dave Smith as one of this year's winners of the National Poetry Series, has absorbed a wide range of influences. The first part of the book is rich with meditations on the natural world, such as "Tarantula," in which the poet invokes Frost while observing a group of boys tormenting a spider: "They are not humbled/by the flawless machinery of its form,/. . . still they fling their crooked stick/to the far weeds and crouch in silence as it/sidles back to the dark that gave it shape." Later Spera turns to the industrial world, with poems that recall, in both their single-stanza form and elegiac tone, the working-man laments of Philip Levine.

Most surprising and effective, though, is the bravado Spera shows in the political poems that make up much of the book's final section. Spera finds a public voice in these poems that is reminiscent of Auden or, more recently, Robert Pinsky, without being merely imitative. He takes on subject matters as daunting as Bosnia and 9/11. Spera's formal skills help him modulate the emotional tenor of "In a Field Outside the Town," which dramatizes a man's survival of a mass murder. The poem constantly turns away from the horror to the pastoral imagery of a regenerative nature, until the dead merge with the landscape they'll become: "the bodies never found, bulldozed into clay" and later, "faces turned like gourds in the dark mire." The poem is powerfully restrained, as is "The Aerialist," which uses the narrative of Frenchman Philippe Petit stringing a wire between the towers of the World Trade Center and walking across to comment obliquely on the 9/11 tragedy.

There's something about formal verse that tends to muffle personality, and too often when young poets turn to form it's an embrace of tradition over individual talent. Here, Spera lets himself be funny at times, sometimes crude, often violent. His verbal flourishes allow the poems to maintain a contemporary feel amidst conventional rhyme schemes. Spera's talent, luckily, is strong enough to endure the force of his influences. (SG)

Cuba Diaries: An American Housewife in Cuba
by Isadora Tattlin
Algonquin, 2002, 308 pp., $24.95

Isadora Tattlin is the pseudonym of an American woman who traveled to Havana in the mid-1990s with her husband, a European businessman, and recorded the everyday struggles of living in Cuba. Her diaries, which span four years, chronicle the severe culture clash Tattlin experienced upon moving to that country from Europe with her two young children. While most of the names and identifying details of the people in the book have been changed or kept intentionally vague to avoid political persecution, Tattlin successfully manages to convey the intimate texture of her life in Cuba, from her ongoing quest for basic foodstuffs in the markets (and black markets) of Havana to her encounters with the other expatriates and eccentrics who populate the odd social circle of foreign businesspeople in the tightly regulated country.

Though we get glimpses of Cuba's political and cultural history, the real story of this book is how one acquires the necessities of life there. Tattlin's prose comes most alive when recording the labyrinthine maneuverings it takes for anyone in Cuba to get anything, whether it be material goods, visas or medical attention. She demonstrates how finagling supplies and services has become an art form, to the point that her cook is an object of both Tattlin's veneration and suspicion for her skill in manipulating the black market.

Tattlin begins the book with an inventory of the massive quantities of canned food, cleaning supplies and paper products that she ships to Havana in preparation for their arrival. From this moment, the record of procurement structures the book, which is a virtual litany of schemes to find things ranging from suitable swimming instructors for the children to edible flour to Fidel Castro's favorite drink for a dinner party she hosts (she is told Chivas Regal, but it turns out to be sweet vermouth; he ends up with white wine). Tattlin reveals just how crucial the most trivial household goods are and how painful and sometimes hilarious it can be to always be searching for them.

Two incidents stand out as epitomizing Tattlin's changing views on Cuba and the world beyond its borders. In the first, she finds the expensive napkins she has shipped from Europe being used as toilet paper in the remote country farmhouse of one of her servants. The moment exposes the unbridgeable rift between her situation and the situation of those who make Cuba their permanent home. In the second incident, Tattlin is overcome with rage when a visitor from the United States neglects to bring Ziplocs in the size she has requested. She fumes, "Not receiving something you need is bad, but receiving something you don't need is somehow worse. . . . Is it not possible for people to imagine that I have spent *two whole weeks* thinking of all of the progress I would be able to make once those things arrived?" As odd as it seems to think that Ziplocs might be crucial to anyone's progress, by the time the book concludes, it makes sense. Tattlin has imparted a new understanding of the way mundane items structure our lives. At the same time, she does an excellent job of painting Cuba through the day-to-day struggle for these items. Though her interactions with the Cubans around her often come off as superficial due to the focus on the goods and services the people supply, they are also infused with a desperation that builds over the four-year period to create a vision of Cuba that feels far more authentic than any of her brief forays into lush description or political analysis. In this way, Tattlin constructs a portrait of a society driven by a grim pattern of gains and losses, a culture she successfully captures because she lives there herself. (TH)

Reviews by: Tom Dillingham, Speer Morgan, Anthony Varallo, Bill Grattan, Scott Sciortino, Michael Piafsky, Patricia Schultheis, Steve Gehrke, Tina Hall

TIN HOUSE MAGAZINE & TIN HOUSE BOOKS
PRESENT THE 2ND ANNUAL

TIN HOUSE
summer writers workshop

A ONE-WEEK
WRITING INTENSIVE

workshops, readings,
seminars, and panels

FICTION
NONFICTION
POETRY
FILM

REED COLLEGE : PORTLAND, OREGON

July 10 to July 18

FACULTY AND GUESTS:
Dorothy Allison . Amy Bartlett . Susan Bell . Aimee Bender . Susan Choi
Charles D'Ambrosio . Denis Johnson . Jeanne McCulloch . Chris Merrill
Oren Moverman . Chris Offutt . Whitney Otto . Dale Peck . Peter Rock
James Salter . Elissa Schappell . Mona Simpson . Mark Strand
Anthony Swofford . Abigail Thomas

SPACE IS LIMITED
For more information and application guidelines: www.tinhouse.com or call 503 219-0622

INKWELL

**The Literary Journal of Manhattanville College's
Master of Arts in Writing Program**

Annual Contests in Fiction and Poetry

Prizes of $1,000 and $1,500 respectively

Our authors have been recognized by

Pushcart Prize XXIII
"Save the Bones for Henry Jones" by Dan Masterson

Best American Essays 2002
"Cars" by Cynthia Anderson ("notable essay")

Visit us at **inkwelljournal.org**

Inkwell Magazine, Manhattanville College
2900 Purchase Street, Purchase, NY 10577 914-323-7239

Subscribe today. One year $8; two years $15

MANHATTANVILLE COLLEGE
Educating ethically and socially responsible leaders since 1841.

independent
innovative
experimental

Fourteen Hills

Summer / Fall
Two Thousand Three
Seven Dollars

Vol. 9, No. 2: Don Waters interviews Stuart David

Forthcoming Vol. 10, No. 1

Rudolph Wurlitzer's libretto to the
Philip Glass opera "In the Penal Colony"
based on the story by Franz Kafka. Fiction
by Nicholas Montemarano, Robert Olmstead,
Mikhail Iossel, Peter Orner, Laird Hunt,
& Stephen Elliot; poetry by Zack Rogow,
Dionisio D. Martínez, Michael S. Harper,
Ed Skoog, Kim Addonizio, & Daniel J.
Langton. Artwork by Chris Johanson.

Recent Contributors

Brian Evenson, Christopher Sorrentino,
Pamela Ryder, Diane Williams, Cooley
Windsor, Fernand Roqueplan, & Carl Phillips

Bambi Holmes Award

$250 to the best poem and best work of prose
by an emerging writer (not yet published
a book at time of publication) printed
each year by Fourteen Hills. Submission
information available at www.14hills.net.

fourteen hills

Fourteen Hills • Department of Creative Writing
1600 Holloway Avenue, San Francisco, CA 94132-1722
hills@sfsu.edu • www.14hills.net

Fourteen Hills: The SFSU Review is committed to publishing contemporary literary art.
It is published twice yearly by the Creative Writing Department at San Francisco State University.

SUBSCRIPTIONS: Single issue (current): $7 • One year (two issues): $12 • Two years (four issues): $21
Institutional (one year): $18 • Back issues as available (please specify): $5

River City -- Summer 2004

announcing

The River City Fiction and Poetry Contests

1st Place Fiction Award $1500

1st Place Poetry Award $1000

go to *www.people.memphis.edu/~rivercity* for details

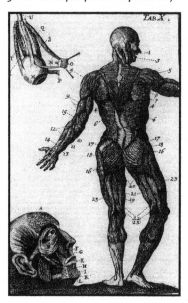

We are also accepting regular submissions of poetry, fiction, essays, and artwork for another non-thematic issue. *The submission deadline is March 15th, 2004.*

Department of English
University of Memphis
Memphis, TN 38152
phone (901) 678-4591
fax (901) 678-2226
rivercity@memphis.edu